THE MEN AT SYLVIA'S DOOR
and
THE "AGENT" WITH DIRTY FINGERNAILS

THE MEN AT SYLVIA'S DOOR
and
THE "AGENT" WITH DIRTY FINGERNAILS

Fifty Years Later, the Florida Keys' Connections to the Warren Commission Report

J. Timothy Gratz and Mark Howell

ABSOLUTELY AMAZING eBOOKS

Published by Whiz Bang LLC, 926 Truman Avenue, Key West, Florida 33040, USA.

The Men at Sylvia's Door and The "Agent" With Dirty Fingernails copyright © 2014, 2015 by J. Timothy Gratz and Mark Howell. Electronic compilation / paperback edition copyright © 2014, 2015 by Whiz Bang LLC. Revised edition.

All rights reserved. No part of this book may be reproduced, scanned, or transmitted in any form or by any means, electronic or mechanical, including photocopying, recording, or any information storage and retrieval system, without permission in writing from the publisher. Please do not participate in or encourage piracy of copyrighted materials in violation of the author's rights. Purchase only authorized ebook editions.

This work is based on factual events. While the author has made every effort to provide accurate information at the time of publication, neither the publisher nor the author assumes any responsibility for errors, or for changes that occur after publication. Further, the publisher does not have any control over and does not assume any responsibility for author or third-party websites or their contents. How the e-book displays on a given reader is beyond the publisher's control.

For information contact
Publisher@AbsolutelyAmazingEbooks.com

ISBN-13: 978-1502597205
ISBN-10: 1502597209

"I think the [Warren] report, to those who have studied it closely, has collapsed like a house of cards ... the fatal mistake the Warren Commission made was not to use its own investigators, but instead to rely on the CIA and FBI personnel, which played directly into the hands of senior intelligence officials who directed the cover-up."

- Richard Schweiker, Senator and former Church Committee member, speaking on *Face the Nation* on June 27, 1976.

THE MEN AT SYLVIA'S DOOR

and

THE "AGENT" WITH DIRTY FINGERNAILS

TABLE OF CONTENTS

PUBLISHER'S NOTE: WHY THIS BOOK?

PREFACE: WHY THE COVER-UP?

INTRODUCTION: HOW THIS BOOK CAME TO BE & GERRY HEMMING

CHAPTER ONE: THE SECRET SERVICE AGENT WITH DIRTY FINGERNAILS

CHAPTER TWO: HEMMING SOLVES THE MYSTERY OF ODIO'S VISITORS BUT THE PLOT THICKENS

CHAPTER THREE: AUGUST 1963 OSWALD ATTEMPTS TO INFILTRATE DRE

CHAPTER FOUR: DECEMBER 1962 OSWALD ATTEMPTS TO INFILTRATE INTERPEN

AFTERWARD: A SERIES OF BOOKS WILL OFFER NEW RESEARCH

APPENDIX: THE WARREN COMMISSION DEPOSITION OF SYLVIA ODIO

Publisher's Note

Many of us remember exactly where we were when we learned of the murder of President John Fitzgerald Kennedy. And a number of us witnessed the killing of accused assassin Lee Harvey Oswald on national TV. What turbulent times for our nation!

For the majority of Americans, the simplistic explanation put forth by the Warren Commission didn't satisfy our instinct that there was more to the story than a lone nut with a cheap rifle. Early researchers pointed to unexplained facts, witness accounts, ignored evidence and a seeming "rush to judgment" – only to be branded as conspiracy crazies.

Time has amassed a widely felt public opinion that the death of President Kennedy was the result of a conspiracy. Today 61% of Americans believe that others besides Lee Harvey Oswald were involved. At times, that percentage has been as high as 81%.

But, really: Whodunit?

Problem is, there were too many suspects: the mob, the Cubans, the anti-Castro factions, the CIA (or rogue elements of it), the Russians, you name them.

Over time however, as more documents were released and investigations continued, a clearer picture emerged.

Now, more than 50 years after the JFK Assassination (as historical shorthand has tagged it), there exist better assessments of what happened on November 22, 1963, in Dallas, Texas.

Despite hundreds and hundreds of book already published on the subject, there's more to be said -- sharper analysis, uncovered details, a better piecing together of the mosaic. Time offers a better perspective, witnesses come forward, the puzzle gets closer to being solved.

That's why we have launched a new book series titled *JFK Assassination Unraveled*.

The Men at Sylvia's Door and The "Agent" With Dirty Fingernails is the first volume in that series.

The idea is to offer easily digestible material rather than overwhelm readers with the epic story of President John F. Kennedy's assassination with all its confusing details and seemingly contradictory facts. We believe these presentations reveal the "false flag" of the Warren Commission and provide you with a greater understanding of this event that changed history.

I recall standing near the fountain on my college campus when I learned of President Kennedy's assassination and remained glued to the TV for days afterwards, witnessing Jack Ruby put an end to the chance to learn the truth from Lee Oswald. Was he a Marxist gone amok? A CIA operative being used as a patsy? A Castro agent on a mission? A mob pawn? A programmed Russian assassin? Or, as we were told by the Warren Commission, simply a lone nut?

I spent years reading all the familiar tomes: *Rush to Judgment* by Mark Lane; *JFK: The CIA, Vietnam And The Plot To Assassinate John F. Kennedy* by L. Fletcher Prouty; *Crossfire* by Jim Marrs; even Vincent Bugliosi's apologia

J. Timothy Gratz and Mark Howell

Reclaiming History. On top of all them were the multiple volumes of the Warren Commission Report. Our bookshelves turned into an entire JFK Assassination library.

Later on I became acquainted with Richard Stolley, the journalist who bought the Zapruder film for Time-Life; I got to know people in common with Tink Thompson, author of *Six Seconds in Dallas*; I became friends with Larry Hancock, author of *Someone Would Have Talked*; I'd hung out with Lamar Waldron, author of *The Hidden History of the JFK Assassination*; I put Pat Speer up in my guest apartment; have clandestine drinks in the Algonquin's Blue Bar with CIA operatives.

Mark Howell and Tim Gratz are two journalists who have been researching the Florida Keys connections to the assassination in much the same way Jim Garrison had uncovered the New Orleans links. Through them I became quite friendly with Gerald Patrick Hemming, the mysterious figure who ran the paramilitary training camp on No Name Key during the aftermath of the Cuban Missile Crisis. Gerry had agreed to allow my production company to film a documentary in which he promised to identify all the participants in the Kennedy assassination. Unfortunately, he died before any of that could happen.

A few years ago, I joined Howell and Gratz in hosting a seminar on the JFK assassination at a local community college. That led to more research on Lee Harvey Oswald, the shooting at Dealey Plaza, and the possible masterminds behind the assassination. The resulting PowerPoint has been presented to numerous civic and law enforcement groups.

JFK Assassination Unraveled: Book I

After a little arm-twisting, I convinced Tim Gratz and Mark Howell to participate in this new book series, *JFK Assassination Unraveled*. Some of it is new research, some new ways of looking at it, but much of it is an easier-to-grasp presentation – story-by-story, incident-by-incident, fact-by-fact, that will help you better understand why this event has been called "the most pivotal moment in American history."

> Shirrel Rhoades
> Publisher
> Absolutely Amazing eBook
> September 24, 2014

J. Timothy Gratz and Mark Howell

ABBREVIATIONS

HSCA for the House Select Committee on Assassinations
INTERPEN Gerry Hemming's anti-Castro organization
WC for the Warren Commission
WCR for the Warren Commission Report

PREFACE
WHY THE COVER UP?

The two "incidents" discussed in this book should make it obvious that the Warren Commission was not out to discover the truth of the assassination. The first chapter deals with a reliable report by a Dallas police officer that there was a man in the parking lot behind the grassy knoll who had false Secret Service credentials. There could be no innocent explanation for this. Yet there was no investigation of the officer's report and the incident is not even discussed in the report of the Warren Commission even though the Smith testimony just cries conspiracy.

The second incident is a report by Sylvia Odio, a Cuban exile living in Dallas, that just two months before the assassination two Hispanics claiming to be anti-Castro activists came to her door with an American who was one of the Hispanics introduced to her as Leon Oswald. After the assassination, she was sure the American who'd been at her door was the man accused of killing the President.

It was the premise of the Warren Commission that the President's killer was a loner and a Castro sympathizer. If he was in fact traveling with two anti-Castro Hispanics, however, that would destroy the central premise of the Commission. To deflect this scenario, the Commission suggested that the exile had been approached by three specific anti-Castro activists, one of whom was an American "who looked like Oswald." The Commission implied that it was simply a case of mistaken identity.

But the Commission closed shop before the FBI had completed its investigation of the Odio incident. Even before the Report was released, the FBI had interviewed the so-called Oswald look-alike who denied ever visiting the lady. And within a week after the Report was issued, the FBI had shown photographs of the three men "identified" in the Report to Odio and she had denied that any of those three had been the men at her door.

Why was the Commission in such a hurry to close shop and not even wait a week or two for the FBI to complete its investigation?

And why was the report of the fake Secret Service agent never investigated?

The only explanation we might offer is that the Commission feared where an investigation of a conspiracy might lead. In order to persuade Chief Justice Earl Warren to head the Commission, President Johnson had told Warren that if an investigation would demonstrate the existence of foreign involvement in the assassination, then such a demonstration would inexorably lead to a war in which forty million Americans would likely be killed.

That Johnson essentially gave Earl Warren such marching orders in order to limit any evidence that might open the door to a conspiracy is the only explanation we can offer as to why the Commission chose not to investigate what Officer Smith saw and chose to close before the FBI had completed its investigation of the Odio story.

INTRODUCTION
HOW THIS BOOK CAME TO BE

Silvia Odio was a Cuban exile living in Dallas who 50 years ago testified to the Warren Commission (WCR) that in late September of 1963 three strangers appeared at her door requesting her assistance with the Cuban exile community in Dallas.

Two of them were Hispanics and one was a white American introduced to her as "Leon Oswald." She refused to help these men. A day or two later, one of the Hispanics called her and attributed to the American they'd introduced as Leon Oswald a violent statement about JFK.

When Silvia Odio saw Oswald on television on the afternoon of the assassination, she says she actually fainted, convinced that the face she'd just seen on the TV screen belonged to the American who'd been at her door only two months earlier.

The WCR dismissed her conclusion. Without explicitly stating so, it implied that the three men at her door were anti-Castro activists, one of whom was an Oswald look-alike. Implicitly, the Report suggested that she simply mistook the Oswald look-alike for Oswald.

But very soon after the Report was issued, the FBI had conclusively demonstrated that none of the three men listed in the WCR had been Odio's visitors, leaving the identity of her visitors a mystery — a mystery that has plagued assassination researchers for forty one years until their identity was finally revealed in 2007 by Gerry Patrick Hemming, the leader of the anti-Castro organization that once operated on a Florida Keys island known as No Name Key and who was closely associated not only with the three men named in the WCR but also with the two Hispanics who did visit her.

This book's co-authors were the first people to whom Hemming revealed the names of Odio's visitors and thus became the first journalists to reveal their identity in print, in a summer 2007 issue of "Solares Hill," the literary supplement to the Key West Citizen (Mark Howell was then editor of "Solares Hill").

The genesis our ultimate involvement with Gerry Hemming began with a call in the summer of 1975 from a Key West business executive to Senator Richard Schweiker of Pennsylvania, a member of the Church Committee of 1975 that investigated the Kennedy assassination. The man offered Schweiker information that was, if true, tantamount to proof of a conspiracy in the assassination.

The caller was George Faraldo, who for many years was the manager of the Key West airport. Today's road into the airport is called Faraldo Circle and the airport fire-fighting facility is named after him. Faraldo told Schweiker that in the summer of 1963 he saw Lee Harvey Oswald waiting in the airport with a group of students going to Cuba. Also present was a man he recognized as Jack Ruby. Any pre-assassination association between Oswald and his eventual killer would certainly be indicative of a conspiracy.

Schweiker sent to Key West a young Senate staffer named Gaeton Fonzi. Fonzi spent a week in Key West interviewing both Faraldo and his wife and searching for ways to validate Faraldo's story.

Fonzi later became an investigator for the House Select Committee on Assassinations (in that capacity he researched the Odio story and wrote the HSCA report on the Odio incident). Later he wrote a well-received book on his work with the HSCA titled *The Last Investigation*. Chapter Seven of *The Last Investigation* is "Searching for Ghosts in Key West" and it summarizes that week in the Keys when he investigated the Faraldo story.

In the summer of 2003, when first reading *The Last Investigation,* I was stunned by the Faraldo story. There had been other reports of sightings of Ruby with Oswald but none by anyone with the credibility of Faraldo. And despite having read thousands of pages and dozens of books about the assassination, he had never before encountered the Faraldo story and was fascinated that proof of a conspiracy may have occurred in a sighting at his adopted city.

Faraldo went to the Key West Citizen with Fonzi to see if the paper may have covered the 1963 flight to Cuba. It had not, and its then-editor Tom Tuell had no knowledge of the story.

I offered to write the story for publication in late November, which would be the fortieth anniversary of the assassination. In pitching the story I mentioned to Tuell that there were other Keys connections, including a Cuban exile who lived in Key West for a year before moving to Tampa, home of Santo Trafficante, Jr., a Mafia kingpin who many believe helped mastermind the assassination. This exile was in Texas the day of the assassination and the next day flew back to Cuba. Tom Tuell authorized the articles and introduced me to Mark Howell, an editor at the Citizen, who helped write and edit the six articles that the Citizen published from November 19 to November 23, 2003.

In 2004 I began reading and posting on a blog about the Kennedy assassination. My views attracted the interest of Hemming.

In the spring of 2006 Mark Howell came to pick me up at my residence on Riviera Drive. (My vehicle had been destroyed by Hurricane Wilma in October of 2005.) Just as Mark arrived my cell phone rang and we were stunned that it was Gerry Hemming calling.

That phone call started a two-year-long association and friendship with Hemming, our communication consisting both of phone calls and e-mails. We spoke at least three times a week, and the e-mails were as frequent as the phone calls. This association was not just about the assassination, we also discussed personal matters. So I was saddened and bereaved upon learning that my friend had died unexpectedly in January of 2008 at his home in Fayetteville, North Carolina.

J. Timothy Gratz
Key West
September 24, 2014
Tim3056008000@hotmail.com

INTRODUCTION DEUX

MARK HOWELL WEIGHS IN

I remember that day in the summer of 2003 when Tom Tuell introduced me to Tim Gratz and we began to put together our series of stories on the Kennedy assassination. When we were working on the Faraldo story we interviewed his widow who lives comfortably in a house on Flagler Street. She told us that to his dying day her husband was certain he had seen both Oswald and Ruby at the Key West airport. A story we published in November 2003 in Solares Hill was about Gerry Hemming and his Interpen group that camped on No Name Key for a year or so. That led to a series of stories on the assassination published in "Solares Hill." One of them was the first identification in print of the visitors to Sylvia Odio. And an important article on the Cuban exile Gilberto Policarpo Lopez was cited as an important clue to the assassinationby author Lamar Waldron in his book "Ultimate Sacrifice."

Through our work together we met Gordon Winslow of Miami, a leading assassination researcher and the webmaster for the Cuban exile website that republished Solares Hill's articles.

- Mark Howell
Key West, FL
September 24, 2014

GERRY PATRICK HEMMING

Gerald Patrick Hemming, who once led an organization of anti-Castro activists he called Interpen, which for about one year camped in the wilds at No Name Key, near Big Pine Island in the Florida Keys, once told a group of assassination researchers in Dallas that he and an associate, arms dealer Mitch Werbell, should have been arrested immediately after the assassination. "When that didn't happen," he joked, "we knew there was going to be a cover-up."

Although he claimed an "alibi" for his whereabouts on that fateful Friday (that he went to visit a newsman in Miami shortly after he heard of the assassination) there are some researchers who are convinced he played a role, perhaps even as one of its masterminds.

Among the researchers who believe Hemming was a conspirator are New York journalist/author a.j. weberman who spent hours interviewing Hemming for his "nodules" on the assassination.

Another writer is Noel Twyman, who also spent hours with Hemming for his book *Bloody Treason*.

Most researchers, however, believe that Hemming was not a conspirator and probably did not have advance knowledge of the plot, while also conceding that after the event he was able to learn a great deal about those behind the assassination. We personally are convinced that his close associate Ray Hargraves (who some called Hemming's "right-hand man") was involved in the conspiracy. Hemming himself thought that another of his associates, Loran Hall, might have been a shooter, using a rifle that once belonged to Hemming. We will cover this story in the second book in this series. Another Interpen member who some think may have been involved was a man named Ron Ponce DeLeon.

Hemming, born in March of 1937, was one of eleven children. He joined the Marine Corp in 1954.

After leaving the Marines, Hemming worked in 1959 with Castro's forces in Cuba, serving as the adjutant at one of the Cuban air force bases, at St. Julian. While there, he claimed he once saved the life of Soviet deputy premier Anastas Mikoyan, by preventing a sniper from shooting him with a rifle from a tower on the air base during an inspection visit.

Disenchanted with Castro, Hemming returned to the United States where he apparently reported to the CIA on what was going on in Cuba.

Although he never claimed to be an official CIA agent, Hemming did claim to be a "singleton," reporting to James Jesus Angleton, the legendary chief of CIA Counterintelligence. Angleton's uncle had been a partner of John McCone who succeeded Allen Dulles as head of the Central intelligence Agency.

Hemming was a natural leader who attracted many who wanted to join his anti-Castro group that he called Interpen. More than six-feet tall, Hemming presented an imposing figure with the rugged good looks of Errol Flynn.

It was claimed that he could fire two semi-automatic rifles simultaneously, one from each hip.

Although he never graduated from high school, Hemming had an encyclopedic grasp of history and an incredible memory. One assassination researcher has described him as "a valedictorian in a guerilla suit." memory.

Some of the episodes he described were could likely be considered disinformation in order to protect himself from those who might do harm to him and to prevent the disclosure of certain information he knew.

Hemming did claim that he had several encounters with Lee Harvey Oswald, one of which we describe in Chapter Four: "Oswald attempts to infiltrate Interpen."

Note: Hemming participated in several extensive telephone interviews with an assassination researcher named Greg Burnham. These can be accessed through this link: http://assassinationofjfk.net/category/gerry-patrick-hemming-tapes/

There are extensive interviews with Hemming in the book *Bloody Treason* by Noel Twyman.

For a series of short vignettes by various authors and researchers on the assassination and the Warren Commission Report, see link below (caveat: we do not agree with all of the opinions expressed in these interviews):
http://www.ctka.net/2013/50_reasons.html

CHAPTER ONE
DALLAS POLICE OFFICER JOE SMITH AND THE SECRET SERVICE AGENT WITH DIRTY FINGERNAILS

Together with several other Dallas police officers, thirty-year-old Joe Marshall Smith was performing traffic control on the corner of Elm and Houston when the shots rang out on that terrible Friday afternoon. Smith was sure the shots came from the direction of the Texas School Book Depository so he immediately headed toward that building, hoping he would get there before the shooter or shooters could escape.

But he never made it to the Depository. As he approached it he was confronted by a lady who was almost in hysterics. "They are shooting the president from the bushes," she cried, pointing to the bushes at the rear of the grassy knoll area. So Smith headed rapidly in the direction the woman had pointed. He was soon joined by a deputy sheriff.

Smith saw a man near a car, parked in the same general direction that the woman had pointed. Smith pulled his gun and approached the man. He felt silly about having drawn gun since he had no reason to suspect the man, so he reholstered his weapon.

The man, dressed in a sports shirt, produced from his pocket Secret Service credentials that he exhibited to Officer Smith and the deputy sheriff. Smith took a brief look at the credentials (he had seen Secret service credentials before), so he handed them back to the man and went back to his search of the area.

Smith was deposed by an attorney for the Warren Commission on July 23, 1964, almost eight months to the day after the assassination. By that time, Smith had learned that there had been no secret service agents stationed on the knoll.

Smith later cursed himself for letting the man go, intuiting that he might well have been a conspirator. After the incident, Smith became bothered because the man he approached did not look like a government agent; he looked more like a mechanic. Even his fingernails were dirty.

But the credentials the man exhibited had satisfied Officer Smith, who was in a hurry to try and catch any fleeing killers.

What gives Smith's interaction with the man a sinister meaning is that there were no Secret Service agents on the grassy knoll. The WCR states:

[The Secret Service agents assigned to the motorcade] remained at their posts during the race to the hospital. None stayed at the scene of the shooting, and none entered the Texas School Book Depository at or immediately after the shooting. Forrest V. Sorrels, special agent in charge of the

Dallas office, was the first Secret Service Agent to return to the scene of the assassination, approximately 20 to 25 minutes after the shots were fired.

The whereabouts all of the Secret Service agents from the Washington detail are found in their individual reports compiled as Warren Commission Exhibit 1024.

Thus it is conclusive that the man who showed Officer Smith Secret Service credentials and declared himself to be a Secret Service agent was an imposter. There is no innocent explanation for a man with false Secret Service credentials on the scene of the assassination. What Smith saw stands by itself as adequate proof of the existence of a conspiracy.

Moreover, Smith was not the only law enforcement officer who reported encountering false Secret Service agents at the site of the assassination. Sergeant D.W. Harkness testified that he went to the rear of the Book Depository only six minutes after the shots rang out in order to ensure the building was sealed. He testified that when he arrived "there were some Secret Service agents there. I did not get them identified. They told me they were Secret Service agents."

Note: *Smith's Warren Commission Testimony is found in Volume 7 of the Warren Commission Hearings, available on-line through the link below. His description of the man looking like a mechanic was given to author Anthony Summers and published in Summer's book "Conspiracy."*

http://mcadams.posc.mu.edu/russ/testimony/smith_j1.htm

The deposition of D.V. Harkness can be found at this link:

JFK Assassination Unraveled: Book I

http://mcadams.posc.mu.edu/russ/testimony/harkness.htm

J. Timothy Gratz and Mark Howell

THE WARREN COMMISSION REPORT IGNORES THE ISSUE OF FAKE SECRET SERVICE AGENTS AT THE SCENE OF THE ASSASSINATION

Earl Warren presents the Warren Commission Report to President Johnson on September 24, 1964.

The Report states:

The Commission has found no evidence that anyone assisted Oswald in planning or carrying out the assassination.

This despite the sworn testimony of a police officer that there was a man in the rear of the grassy knoll showing Secret Service credentials and another officer testified he encountered men claiming to be Secret Service agents at the rear of the Texas School Book Depository – while other

Commission evidence demonstrated there were no Secret Service agents at the scene of the assassination as all had remained with the motorcade. There is no explanation for a fake Secret Service agent on the knoll or fake agents behind the Texas School Book Depository is compelling evidence of a conspiracy.

Perhaps the first public discussion of the fake Secret Service agent came in an August 1, 1966 article in Greater Philadelphia magazine by then journalist Gaeton Fonzi ("The Warren Commission, the Truth and Arlen Specter") a brilliant critique of the WC. It came out about one month before the publication of Mark Lane's *Rush to Judgment*.

(Fonzi later became an assassination researcher investigator, first for the Church Committee and later for the House Select Committee on Assassinations. As noted in the Introduction.

Here is how an early WC critic, Sylvia Meagher, describes the Smith and Harkness incidents in her 1967 book "Accessories After the Fact" (one of the best early criticisms of the Commission; the 1992 edition of the book has a preface by then Senator Richard Schweiker, who as a member of the Church Committee received the report by the former manager of the Key West airport that he had seen Ruby and Oswald together in the summer of 1963).

"Few mysteries in the case are as compelling as this one, and it is appalling that the Commission ignored or failed to recognize the grounds for serious suspicion of a well-organized conspiracy at work, It seems inconceivable that none of the many investigators and lawyers saw the significance of the reports made by these witnesses or realized that assassins positioned on the grassy knoll -- behind the fences or the trees -- might have been armed with forged secret service credentials and lost themselves in the crowd that surged into the area."

Larry Hancock, a leading writer on the assassination, suggests an answer to how the Commission could have made such an oversight. Perhaps, he suggested in an e-mail to the authors, none of the Commissioners had read Smith's deposition. None were present at his deposition.

There are seventeen volumes of Commission testimony and there were 552 witnesses deposed.

In his 1966 article in Greater Philadelphia magazine, Fonzi pointed out:

The [WC] staff lawyers had to decide which witnesses ... should be brought to testify before formal hearings of the Commission (only 94 of the 552 who provided testimony finally were), and what questions needed further investigation and what details were relevant or irrelevant.

At least two Commission staffers, assistant counsel Wesley Liebeler, who took Officer Smith's deposition, and deputy counsel David W. Belin, who took the deposition of Sergeant Harkness, had to be aware of the problem with persons at the scene of the assassination falsely claiming to be Secret Service agents. But neither Officer Smith nor Sgt. Harkness were designated by staff as important witnesses whose testimony should be heard in formal hearings before the Commission. And presumably staff counsel never advised the Commissioners that the issue of people at the site of the assassination falsely claiming to be Secret Service agents deserved further investigation.

It cannot be determined at this point whether staff counsel simply made independent decisions to withhold this critical evidence or if they were directed by senior counsel or even a member of the Commission. One explanation might be that the possibility of a foreign conspiracy was still considered and that there was concern that a foreign conspiracy if revealed could well lead to a horrific World War.

J. Timothy Gratz and Mark Howell

THE HOUSE SELECT COMMISSION ON ASSASSINATIONS ATTEMPTS TO RESOLVE THE SMITH STORY

According to the Final Report of the House Select Committee on Assassinations:

"The Committee made an effort to identify the man who talked to Patrolman Smith.

... the Committee did obtain evidence that military intelligence personnel may have identified themselves as Secret Service agents, or they may have been misidentified as such. Robert E. Jones, a retired Army lieutenant colonel who in 1963 was commanding officer of the military intelligence region that encompassed Texas, told the Committee that from 8 to 12 military intelligence personnel in plain clothes were assigned to Dallas to provide supplemental security for the President's visit. He indicated that these agents had identification credentials and, if questioned, would have most likely have stated that they were on detail to the Secret Service.

The Committee sought to identify these agents so they could be questioned. The Department of Defense indicated, however, that a search of its files showed "no records . . . indicating any Department of Defense Protective Services in Dallas." The Committee was unable to resolve the contradiction.

As noted below, we think the man Smith encountered was identified in 1967 by a man named William Acker. However, the FBI report on its interview with William Acker was never presented to the HSCA by the FBI so the HSCA did not know that there was a man who a) had expressed anti-Kennedy statements; b) was said to be in Dallas at least around the time of the assassination; and c) had false Secret Service credentials in his possession, together with many weapons. Had the HSCA known this it could have subpoenaed the man (we name him below) to testify (he died in 2002). If he was still alive, Officer Smith could have been present to see if he could identify him).

J. Timothy Gratz and Mark Howell

THE REPORT OF WILLIAM ACKER OF AN ANTI-CASTRO ACTIVIST WITH FALSE SECRET SERVICE CREDENTIALS AND WEAPONS

Several years after the assassination, the FBI came close to apprehending the man who falsely claimed to be a Secret Service agent but for the reasons indicated below, it failed to follow that lead.

On January 10, 1967 an FBI agent interviewed a William Blanton Acker. The file is only labeled "JFK Suspect" and it was first released in 1993.

Here is what Acker told the FBI (emphasis supplied):

In 1963 he was in Miami, Florida employed at the Royal Castle Number 2, Flagler and Second, and met one Art Silva. Art Silva at the time was living with one Phyllis (LNU) at a small hotel across the street from [the Royal Castle]. They later moved to an apartment in a court near Lejeune Road and Eighth Street... One of their neighbors in the court (consisting of about ten units) was one Roy (LNU) who was living with some woman, name unrecalled, in the court next door to Art Silva. Roy, according to Art Silva, had several telescopic sight rifles, grenades, mortars, dynamite, etc. in his room. Also, Roy had made a trip to Dallas, Texas in late 1963 and *was reported by Art Silva to have Secret Service credentials.* Roy was also associated with various Cuban resistance movements and was an ex-Marine. William Acker also notes that the article he read says a policeman stopped a man in Dallas who has secret service credentials.

Speculation: it may well have been this article about the Smith encounter that prompted Acker to call the FBI.

Acker says that in late 1963 he met Art Silva in an open air sandwich shop in Miami for a beer and Art Silva talked of his next-door neighbor Roy and said Roy was working with the Cubans and would help get Acker into the movement if he wanted to help out in winning Cuba back from Castro ... Acker says at a Christmas party in 1963 he was arguing with Roy and almost came to blows as Roy blamed President Kennedy personally for the death of one of his friends who was in the Bay of Pigs invasion. Acker also claimed that Silva had told him "Roy is into something big ... the biggest thing this country has seen." Acker says he thought Silva was talking about a robbery or something of that sort because he suspected Silva of being mixed up with various underworld characters. At this time Acker thinks it was the assassination of President Kennedy after reading the article in the Post of January 14. [Presumably this is the article where Acker read about Officer Joe Smith's encounter with the fake Secret Service agent.

Through an investigation the FBI learned the identity of the man with the weapons cache and the Secret Service credentials. Our story continues:

The FBI found that the tax records of Royal Castle indicated that an A.A. Silva had worked at Royal Castle until September 1963, and at that time resided at 207 N.E. 2d Ave (which turned out to be a fictitious address). William Acker was employed at the same Royal Castle until December 1963.

When the FBI checked an apartment in a court, Mrs. Katherine W. Drobat told them that a man named Roy E Hargraves had managed the place when she owned the cottages and also when Mrs. Nees had them. She advised that Hargraves was a petty thief and involved in gun running and in Cuban affairs. He was later dismissed from the job.

Thus although the FBI agents involved in interviewing Acker surely must have known the significance of the fact that, according to Silva per Acker, Hargraves possessed false Secret Service credentials, it never bothered to interview him. Nor did the FBI locate and interview Art Silva.

The FBI stated its reasons for its discontinuation of its investigation into Acker's claim: "For the information of the Bureau, complete facts concerning the involvement of Hargraves in Cuban affairs can be found in [two] cases [whose names we omit for space considerations]. In view of the fact that this investigation is predicated on information furnished by William Blanton Acker, *an individual with a diseased mind,* and also because a reliable source [Interpen member Howard K. Davis] advised that Hargraves was in Miami from November 1963 to March 1964 engaged in Cuban activities, no further action is being taken at Miami." [Emphasis supplied.]

Here is the info on Acker's "diseased mind": He was voluntarily admitted to a VA Hospital in September 14, 1958 and released on November 7, 1958. His discharge diagnosis stated: "Schizophrenic reaction, paranoid type. Manifested by circumstantiality, flight of ideas, etc., moderate. He was considered competent upon discharge." That he spent several weeks in a mental institute nine years before his report to the FBI does not seem an adequate reason to summarily dismiss his report, if true of obvious importance to one of the nation's greatest tragedies. And who says that an incompetent person can never provide accurate information?

Moreover much of his information was not based on his own observations of Hargraves but on observations made by Silva and reported to him by Silva, e.g., Hargraves' weapons cache and his forged Secret Service credentials. How could the FBI evaluate that information without talking to Silva himself?

And regarding Davis' alleged statement to the FBI concerning Hargraves' whereabouts in November 1963 through March of 1963, that of course was irrelevant. The only relevant information was whether Hargraves was in Dallas on November 22nd. There is no information in the file that Davis could supply Hargraves with an alibi for that critical date. And since Davis was close to Hargraves, he could have been lying to protect his friend or even because Davis himself was part of the conspiracy (although we do not think he was).

And as noted below, in 2007 Hargraves admitted to an author that he was in fact in Dallas on November 22nd. Again, why did the FBI not personally quiz Hargraves about his whereabouts on November 22 rather than relying on the memory of a third person?

Parenthetically, as noted in Chapter Two, in connection with its investigation of the Odio incident, the FBI had, in the summer of 1964, interviewed three of Hargraves' associates from Interpen: Loran Hall; Larry Howard and William Seymour. Some suspect that Hall may have been involved in the assassination, but there is no reason to suspect either Howard or Seymour.

Imagine what might have happened if the FBI had interviewed Hargraves in 1967; if it had determined if Officer Smith was able to identify Hargraves as the man he had encountered on the knoll on November 22nd. Arguably that would have been sufficient to indict Hargraves as an accessory to murder. Had Hargraves been faced with the death penalty, he might well have disclosed others who were involved in the plot. The conspiracy could have unraveled in 1967.

JFK Assassination Unraveled: Book I

WHO WAS ROY HARGRAVES?

Felipe Vidal Santiago   Roy Hargraves

THE NO NAME KEY ASSASSIN IN DALLAS ON A DEADLY MISSION

Roy E. Hargraves, age 33 in 1963, was a member of Hemming's Interpen organization that camped for several months on No Name Key. He was a close associate of Hemming; some described Hargraves as Hemming's "right-hand man."

Thanks to a disclosure by Hemming, we know the deadly role Hargraves played in the assassination. He was prepared to blow up the entire presidential limousine to guarantee the death of the president.

As noted below, Hargraves told author Noel Twyman that he flew with Felipe Vidal Santiago on a private plane flew from Miami to Dallas on Monday, November 18th and they flew back to Miami on the evening of the 22nd. He told Twyman that Vidal was the person on Elm Street with the walkie-talkie.

Hargraves was an expert in explosives. And he was a violent man. Some stories state that he would open the door of a residence and throw in a hand grenade.

According to Hemming, Hargraves had constructed a huge bomb that had been planted in a car that was then parked near the exit to Dealey Plaza. The bomb was to be used as a last resort, to ensure that JFK did not leave Dealey Plaza alive. Had the shooting been aborted for any reason, or had the conspirators not been convinced that one of the shots had been fatal, the bomb would have been detonated as the presidential limousine sped by it. The bomb was powerful enough that it would have destroyed the limousine and every one in it, including Mrs. Kennedy, the Connallys and the two Secret Service agents.

Here is what Larry Hancock wrote about the car bomb in his 2011 book "Nexus": "We do know, from photographs that a number of vehicles were parked on the side of the access lane used to enter Stemmons Freeway from Elm Street."

Hancock has written two books on the assassination of President Kennedy and for over a decade he served as the conference speaker and chair of the November in Dallas research conferences sponsored by JFK Lancer. In "Nexus" Hancock strongly implies that he believes that Hargraves was the man with the false Secret Service credentials that Officer Smith encountered only minutes after the assassination.

Significantly, Hargraves admitted to author Noel Twyman ("Bloody Treason" 1997) that he had been in Dallas and had indeed constructed a bomb although he claimed that he did not have knowledge of the intended use of the bomb.

Below is a memo, published in the 2010 eBook version of "Bloody Treason," that Twyman made memorializing his 2001 interview with Hargraves:

DATE: February 10, 2001

Roy [Hargraves] now admits that he went from Miami to Dallas with Vidal on November 18, 1963 and returned to Miami on the afternoon/evening of November 22. They flew by private jet both ways. There were others, unnamed with them on the plane. Roy would not reveal who provided the plane. Roy would not say what he did in Dallas, or whom he met there. Roy said that he did not shoot JFK, didn't even know that JFK was to be in Dallas.

At the end of the meeting when we were looking at photos of Dealey Plaza from Groden's book of photos, Roy reiterated that Vidal was the man on Elm Street with the walkie-talkie. I asked Roy if he was speculating on this. He said no, he was not speculating. He said compare Vidal's photo to the Saturday Evening Post photos. He explained that Vidal did not know what was coming down and was following specific instructions to do exactly specific things, thus explaining Vidal's arms being raised up.

Roy said it was Colonel William Bishop who ordered Vidal to come to Dallas at that time and that it was under Vidal's instructions that Roy come along.

The Vidal to whom Hargraves referred was a Cuban exile named Felipe Vidal Santiago. He was so close to Hemming that Hemming named his first-born son Felipe.

Vidal was arrested with three others when they attempted to penetrate Cuba in March of 1964. All four were executed in April of 1964 (per a May 28, 1964 story in the Miami Times.) At a conference of assassination researchers and writers in Havana in December of 1997, Cuban intelligence officer Fabian Escalante stated that before his death Vidal told his interrogators that Col. William Bishop had invited him to a meeting in Dallas in November of 1963, to discuss anti-Castro activities. Although we do not credit everything that Escalante says, it is interesting that he reported in 1997 that Vidal claimed that this Col. Bishop invited him to Dallas, and the Bishop "invitation" was confirmed by Hargraves to Twyman in February of 2001.

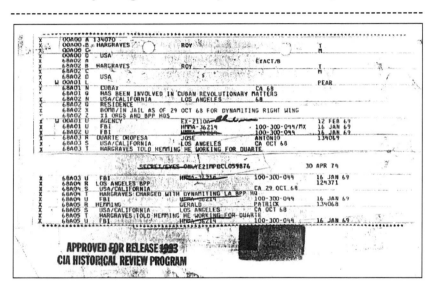

J. Timothy Gratz and Mark Howell

THE ULTIMATE IRONY: OLIVER STONE EMPLOYS ONE OF THE ASSASSINS AS A CONSULTANT TO HIS "JFK" MOVIE

Oliver Stone directing Kevin Costner on the set of "JFK" in 1992.

Hargraves and Hemming were involved in what surely classifies as one of the biggest ironies of the assassination investigation. They were recruited by Oliver Stone to serve (along with fellow Interpen member Howard Davis) as consultants for his movie "JFK," the movie that galvanized the public to the Kennedy conspiracy and led to the JFK Records Act that opened to the public many records relating to the assassination.

Their names are listed in the credits to "JFK." Hemming even has an uncredited part in the movie. He plays the unidentified conspirator who directed the three marksmen to start shooting via a walkie-talkie.

Thus, Stone employed one of the conspirators in his movie about a JFK conspiracy.

Hemming told this author that Stone once overheard a remark by Hargraves that caused Stone to suspect that Hargraves was probably a conspirator. And Stone was concerned about Hemming as well when Hemming urged him to use a black actor as a spotter in the Dal Tex Building. Stone worried that Hemming knew too much and that he might have also have been a conspirator. According to Hemming, Stone immediately turned ashen and he never spoke to them again.

Hemming did tell us that a black Cuban exile was the spotter in the Dal Tex Building.

HEMMING AND JIM GARRISON

Stone's movie focused on the investigation of New Orleans DA Jim Garrison into the Kennedy assassination and his unsuccessful prosecution of businessman Clay Shaw as a conspirator. There is a Garrison connection to the No Name Key Interpen group. It has been reported that when Garrison first started his investigation he believed the assassination had been planned and practiced on No Name Key. In a maneuver no doubt designed to deflect any investigation into his Interpen operation, Hemming walked into Garrison's office and offered to help his investigation. Given the role Hemming's friend Hargraves played in the conspiracy, Hemming's maneuver may have prevented the exposure of Hargraves' role and thus the unraveling of the conspiracy by Garrison as early as 1967.

Parenthetically, like many other assassination researchers this writer doubts that Clay Shaw, the man Garrison unsuccessfully tried as a Kennedy conspirator, played any role in the assassination. Some even believe that the Garrison probe was intended to deflect scrutiny from the role of New Orleans mafia "don" Carlos Marcello, a man who hated the Kennedys and who, while incarcerated in a federal penitentiary in the 1980s for his role in the Brilab scandal "confessed" his participation in the assassination to a fellow inmate who reported it to the FBI. The Marcello confession is detailed in the 2013 book *The Hidden History of the Kennedy Assassination* by LaMar Waldron. Marcello's involvement was first probed at length in the 1989 book

Mafia Kingfish: Carlos Marcello and the Assassination of JFK, written by John Davis, a cousin of Jacqueline Kennedy.

There are several reports that Robert F. Kennedy was convinced of Marcello's involvement in his brother's murder, including a statement by Jack Newfield, who produced a 1998 Discovery Channel documentary on RFK:

"Bobby told [JFK adviser] Arthur Schlesinger he blamed 'that guy in New Orleans' – which meant [Mob boss] Carlos Marcello. Bobby was intense about prosecuting Marcello as attorney general. He deported him in 1961, indicted him when he returned, and tried him in 1963."

In another irony of the assassination, Marcello was acquitted of the charges against him on November 22, 1963. That was a good day for the bad guys.

For ebook readers, you can visit this site to view many FBI documents regarding Hargraves, including the Acker report on Hargraves. You will need to scroll down to find it but there are numerous FBI files re Hargraves here.
http://www.scribd.com/doc/231956132/Roy-Emery-Hargraves

Let us pause now to consider what this story tells us about the assassination. It tells us how well organized it was. The organizers had supplied the conspirators on the scene with fake Secret Service credentials so they could avoid scrutiny while making their escape. And they had created the car bomb as a back up to ensure that the President did not leave Dealey Plaza alive.

CHAPTER TWO

FORTY YEARS LATER HEMMING SOLVES THE MYSTERY OF THE ODIO'S VISITORS
DISCUSSING THE PURPORTED KEYS' CONNECTION TO THE "ODIO INCIDENT"
PER THE WARREN COMMISSION

In the Introduction we briefly described what has become known as "the Odio incident." Sylvia Meagher, author of "Accessories After the Fact," one of the earliest books critical of the Warren commission, characterized the Odio incident as "proof of the plot," i.e., that there was indeed a plot (conspiracy) to kill the president. David Kaiser, a military historian and author of the 2008 book "The Road to Dallas," calls the Odio incident "the single most important piece of evidence in the case." We argue below that the Odio incident is not necessarily proof of any plot and is far from the most important evidence in the case (we think the Smith incident described in the first Chapter could well qualify for that distinction). Nevertheless the Odio incident merits serious consideration, and in particular the strange role played by Loran Hall, who Hemming believed might have been one of the shooters in Dallas.

First we discuss at greater length the basics of the "Odio incident." Then we discuss how the Warren Commission handled it by assigning responsibility to three men from Hemming's Interpen organization. Then we discuss whether the Odio incident constituted "proof of the plot" as many argue.

THE ODIO INCIDENT:

SYLVIA ODIO

It is significant to note that Sylvia Odio did not contact the authorities over the strange encounter she claimed she had had with Lee Harvey Oswald in late September of 1963. Rather, the FBI contacted her because of a report the FBI had received from Mrs. Lucille Connell, a lady active in the Dallas Catholic Church Cuban Relief Committee. Connell reported that her friend Silvia Odio had told her she had seen Lee Harvey Oswald speaking to a group of anti-Castro Cuban exiles and that Oswald was "brilliant and clever"; but, per Connell, Odio also told her that she had heard indirectly from a Cuban source in New Orleans that Oswald was suspected of being a double agent.

There is no record that Oswald ever spoke to any exile group in Dallas but when the FBI contacted Odio several weeks later (on December 18, 1963) she told them an even more intriguing story about a strange encounter she'd had with three men, one of who she was convinced was Oswald, an encounter less than two months before the assassination.

Odio was an extremely attractive divorcee, a mother of six, who lived on Magellan Circle in Dallas. Her parents had been wealthy Cuban business owners but they were imprisoned in Cuba because they had harbored on their large estate a man who had been involved in a 1961 attempt to assassinate Castro, an attempt organized by Antonio Veciana, a man who plays an important role in a story we will examine in the second book of this series.

Silvia and her husband had left Cuba for Puerto Rico after her parents were imprisoned but they separated after a short time. Silvia moved to Dallas where her two sisters Sarita and Annie were living. She was associated with an exile group called JURE, headed by a man called Manuel Ray. (Her parents had been associated with Manuel Ray's earlier group, the MRP.)

Here is what Odio told the two FBI agents who interviewed her in December of 1963:

... In late September or early October 1963, two Cuban men came to her house and stated they were from JURE. They were accompanied by an individual whom they introduced as LEON OSWALD. Miss Odio stated that based upon photographs she had seen of LEE HARVEY OSWALD she is certain that [the man introduced to her as LEON OSWALD is identical with LEE HARVEY OSWALD.

... Miss Odio stated the purpose of their visit was to ask her to write letters to some various businesses in Dallas and request funds for JURE.

Miss Odio stated that both of her parents are presently in prison in Cuba and for this reason she declined [to help write the letters for fear her parents would be possibly harmed. These two individuals together with Oswald then left. A few days later one of the two Cuban individuals contacted her and stated they were leaving town, presumably to return to either Miami, Florida or Puerto Rico, the headquarters of JURE. The individual who called Miss Odio who only gave his name as LEOPOLDO stated he was not going to have anything further to do with LEON OSWALD since he considered him to be "loco" ... LEOPOLDO stated that OSWALD did not appear sincere. He told them he was an ex-marine and could help them in the underground however he appeared to be very cynical and seemed to think that all Cubans hated all Americans.

According to Leopoldo, OSWALD stated "I'll bet you Cubans could kill Kennedy for what he did to you at the Bay of Pigs."

After the assassination, when Odio saw televised photos of Lee Harvey Oswald, the accused assassin of the president, she fainted and had to be hospitalized because she was certain that Oswald had been the American with the two Hispanics who had come knocking on her door.

The Warren Commission did not depose Odio until July 22, 1964, more than seven months after her FBI interview and only two months before the scheduled deadline for the Commission to "close." Prior to that time, however, the Secret Service had re-interviewed Mrs. Connell. In April Warren Commission deputy counsel Burt Griffin interviewed Miss Odio's psychiatrist who repeated to Griffin (as he had earlier done to the FBI agent who had interviewed Odio) that he believed Odio's story. (She had described the incident to him before the assassination.) The psychiatrist also mentioned that Odio stated she had seen Oswald more than once.

The Odio Warren Commission deposition is appended at the end of this book. It was conducted by deputy counsel Wesley Liebeler. Readers will remember he was the counsel who deposed Officer Smith.

In her deposition, Odio described the two Hispanics who came to her door with the man she later identified as Oswald. She said the American they introduced her to as Leon Oswald had a considerable growth of beard. She stated that one of her sisters, Annie, had opened the door and spoke briefly to the man who called himself Leopoldo. The other man called himself Angelo, she thought.

She testified that Leopoldo, who did most of the talking, tried to establish their bona fides by claiming they were "very good friends" of her father (recall he was still imprisoned in Cuba). She said this struck her as odd because she did not think her father, who had been a successful businessman before his imprisonment, would have friends like the two at her door who she described as "seedy-looking." The man calling himself Leopoldo "gave me so many details about where they saw my father and what activities he was in. I mean, they [he?] gave me almost incredible details about things that somebody who knows him really well would or that somebody informed well knows."

Odio asked Leopoldo if they had been sent by local or national JURE headquarters and when they said no she became suspicious of them. She declined their request for help.

The next evening Odio received a call from "Leopoldo." She stated that he was "trying to get fresh with me" and he told her how pretty she was. To quote her deposition:

Then he said, "What do you think of the American?" And I said, "I don't think anything. And he said "You know it is our ideas to introduce him to the underground in Cuba, because he is great, he is kind of nuts." ... [Leopoldo stated that Leon said that Cubans don't have any guts ... because President Kennedy should have been assassinated after the Bay of Pigs, and some Cubans should have done that [shot Kennedy] because he was the one that was holding the freedom of Cuba actually."

[Leopoldo went on]: And [Leon] said "It is so easy to do it." He had told us.

She also testified that Leopoldo told her several times that Leon was an expert marksman. And he said: "We probably won't have anything to do with him. He is kind of loco."

As we discuss below, questions remain whether the American at Odio's door was really Oswald or an Oswald imposter. (Most researchers believe it was indeed Oswald and so said Hemming.) But there is no way to determine if Oswald in fact made the statements attributed to him by Leopoldo. We later discuss why Leopoldo may have chosen to repeat Oswald's alleged remarks to Odio.

The Odio incident presented a real dilemma for the Warren Commission. Its thesis was that Oswald was, if not a Communist, at a minimum a Castro sympathizing "loner." What then was he doing associating with two anti-Castro

J. Timothy Gratz and Mark Howell

Cubans? And denigrating Kennedy for "holding the freedom of Cuba in his hands"?

THE WARREN COMMISSION USES (DISHONESTLY) THREE HEMMING NO NAME KEY ASSOCIATES TO EXPLAIN THE ODIO INCIDENT

Five weeks after the Odio deposition, on August 29, 1964 Warren Commission Chief Counsel J. Lee Rankin wrote to J. Edgar Hoover urging him to investigate Odio's story more thoroughly. It had to be somehow discredited for the Warren Commission's portrayal of Oswald as a left-leaning "loner nut" was to survive. Rankin knew that and Hoover must have also.

On September 2, just two weeks and two days away from the Warren Commission completion deadline, and five days after the Rankin letter, Hoover wrote his Dallas office stating that it was "highly improbable, if not impossible" for Oswald to have been in Dallas any day between September 24 through the 26th (when he was supposedly en route to his famous trip to Mexico City). Hoover ordered his agents to investigate Odio's "mental status" and her "reputation for veracity."

The results were mixed. Three anti-Castro activists in Dallas belittled her story, but Manolo Ray, the head of JURE, as well as his assistant Cisneros characterized her as intelligent, dedicated, of good character and they considered it unlikely that she had fabricated the story.

On September 16, only eight days before the release date for the Warren Commission Report, Dallas FBI agents discovered that two anti-Castro activists, Loran Eugene Hall and William Seymour, had been in Dallas around the time of the Odio incident. They had been stopped by Dallas police on the way to Florida from California. Both Hall and Seymour had been associated with Hemming's Interpen group and Seymour had lived with Hemming on No Name Key. (As discussed in Chapter Four, Seymour was one of the men arrested with Hemming in Marathon on December 3, 1962, before they were to leave for Cuba.) When arrested in Dallas, Hall and Seymour were hauling a trailer full of arms intended for future incursions into Cuba.

Hall had gone to Cuba shortly after Castro seized control of the island. He was arrested and imprisoned and he shared a cell at Castro's Trescornia prison with Mafia leader Santo Trafficante, who many believe was involved in the plot to kill Kennedy. (Bizarre sidebar here is that Trafficante claimed to have met Kennedy in December of 1957 when then-Senator Kennedy visited Cuba with his friend Senator George Smathers of Florida. One author has claimed that on that trip Trafficante provided prostitutes for Kennedy for a "threesome.")

Hall was released from Trescornia in 1960 and upon his return to the U.S. he was interviewed by the FBI (but not the CIA). Little is known about his activities in the U.S. until late 1962 when he connected with Gerry Hemming in Los Angeles. In early 1963 Hall drove with Hemming back to Florida, stopping over in Dallas to meet with Lester Logue, a wealthy oil geologist, General Edwin Walker and Walker's attorney Robert Morris.

THE WARREN COMMISSION IMPLIES THAT THE MAN ODIO IDENTIFIED AS OSWALD WAS ANTI-CASTRO ACTIVIST WILLIAM SEYMOUR

William Seymour, Dennis Harber, Isidro Borja and Bernardo De Torres

ABOVE, SEYMOUR IS PICTURED (AT LEFT) WITH BERNARDO E TORRES (AT RIGHT) WHOM HEMMING IDENTIFIED AS ONE OF ODIO'S VISITORS)

Below is the entirety of what the Warren Commission Report stated about the Odio incident in its Report, which was released on September 24, 1964:

Alleged association with various Mexican or Cuban individual –That the Commission has examined Oswald's known or alleged contacts and activities in an effort to ascertain whether or not he was involved in any conspiracy may be seen in the investigation it conducted as a result of the testimony given by Mrs. Sylvia Odio. The Commission investigated her statements in connection with its consideration of the testimony of several witnesses suggesting that Oswald may have been seen in the company of unidentified persons of Cuban or Mexican background. Mrs. Odio was born in Havana in 1937 and remained in Cuba until 1960; it appears that both of her parents are political prisoners of the Castro regime. Mrs. Odio is a member of the Cuban Revolutionary Junta (JURE), an anti-Castro organization. She testified that late in September 1963, three men came to her apartment in Dallas and asked her to help them prepare a letter soliciting funds for JURE activities. She claimed that the men, who exhibited personal familiarity with her imprisoned father, asked her if she were "working in the underground," and she replied that she was not. She testified that two of the men appeared to be Cubans, although they also had some characteristics that she associated with Mexicans. Those two men did not state their full names, but identified themselves only by their fictitious underground "war names." Mrs. Odio remembered the name of one of the Cubans as "Leopoldo." The third man, an American, allegedly was introduced to Mrs. Odio as "Leon Oswald," and she was told that he was very much interested in the Cuban cause. Mrs. Odio said that the men told her that they had just come from New Orleans and that they were then about to leave on a trip. Mrs. Odio testified that the next day Leopoldo called her on the telephone and told her that it was his idea to introduce the American into the underground "because he is great, he is kind of nuts." Leopoldo also said that the American had been in the Marine Corps and was an excellent shot, and that the American said the Cubans "don't have any guts ... because President

Kennedy should have been assassinated after the Bay of Pigs, and some Cubans should have done that, because he was the one that was holding the freedom of Cuba actually."

Although Mrs. Odio suggested doubts that the men were in fact members of JURE, she was certain that the American who was introduced to her as Leon Oswald was Lee Harvey Oswald. Her sister, who was in the apartment at the time of the visit by the three men, and who stated that she saw them briefly in the hallway when answering the door, also believed that the American was Lee Harvey Oswald. By referring to the date on which she moved from her former apartment, October 1, 1963, Mrs. Odio fixed the date of the alleged visit on the Thursday or Friday immediately preceding date, i.e., September 26 or 27. She was positive that the visit occurred prior to October 1.

During the course of its investigation, however, the Commission concluded that Oswald could not have been in Dallas on the evening of either September 26 or 27, 1963. It also developed considerable evidence that he was not in Dallas at any time between the beginning of September and October 3, 1963. On April 24, Oswald left Dallas for New Orleans, where he lived until his trip to Mexico City in late September and his subsequent return to Dallas. Oswald is known to have been in New Orleans as late as September 23, 1963, the date on which Mrs. Paine and Marina Oswald left New Orleans for Dallas. Sometime between 4 p.m. on September 24 and 1 p.m. on September 25, Oswald cashed an unemployment compensation check at a store in New Orleans; under normal procedures this check would not have reached Oswald's postal box in New Orleans until at least 5 on September 25. The store at which he cashed the check did not open until 8 a.m. Therefore, it appeared that Oswald's presence in New Orleans until sometime between 8 a.m. and 1 p.m. on September 25 was quite firmly established.

Although there is no firm evidence of the means by which Oswald traveled from New Orleans to Houston, on the first leg of his Mexico City trip, the Commission noted that a Continental Trailways bus leaving New Orleans at 12:30 p.m. on September 25 would have brought Oswald to Houston at 10:50 p.m. that evening. His presence on this bus would be consistent with other evidence before the Commission. There is strong evidence that on September 26, 1963, Oswald traveled on Continental Trailways bus No. 5133 which left Houston at 2:35 a.m. for Laredo, Tex. Bus company records disclose that one ticket from Houston to Laredo was sold during the night shift on September 25-26, and that such ticket was the only one of its kind sold in the period of September 24 through September 26. The agent who sold this ticket has stated that Oswald could have been the purchaser. Two English passengers, Dr. and Mrs. John B. McFarland, testified that they saw Oswald riding alone on this bus shortly after they awoke at 6 a.m. The bus was scheduled to arrive in Laredo at 1:20 p.m. on September 26, and Mexican immigration records show that Oswald in fact crossed the border at Laredo to Nuevo Laredo, Mexico, between 6 a.m. and 2 p.m. on that day. Evidence set out in appendix XIII establishes that Oswald did not leave Mexico until October 3, and that he arrived in Dallas the same day.

The Commission noted that the only time not strictly accounted for during the period that Mrs. Odio The Commission noted that the only time not strictly accounted for during the period that Mrs. Odio thought Oswald might have visited her is the span between the morning of September 25 and 2:35 a.m. on September 26. The only public means of transportation by which Oswald could have traveled from New Orleans to Dallas in time to catch his bus from Houston to Laredo, would have been the airlines. Investigation disclosed no indication that he flew between these points. Moreover, it did not seem probable that Oswald would speed from New Orleans, spend a short time talking to Sylvia Odio, and then travel from Dallas to Mexico City and back on the bus. Automobile travel in the time available, though perhaps possible, would have been difficult. The Commission noted, however, that if Oswald had reached Dallas on the evening of September 25, he could have traveled by bus to Alice, Tex., and there caught the bus which had left Houston for Laredo at 2:35 a.m. on September 26, 1963. Further investigation in that regard indicated, however, that no tickets were sold, during the period September 23-26, 1963 for travel from Dallas to Laredo or points beyond by the Dallas office of Continental Trailways, the only bus line on which Oswald could have made connections with the bus on which he was later seen. Furthermore, if Oswald had traveled from Dallas to Alice, he would not have reached the Houston to Laredo bus until after he was first reportedly observed on it by the McFarlands. Oswald had also told passengers Oswald had also told passengers on the bus to Laredo that he had traveled from New Orleans by bus, and made no mention of an intervening trip to Dallas. In addition, the Commission noted evidence that on the evening of September 25, 1963, Oswald made a telephone call to a party in Houston proposing to visit a resident of Houston that evening and the fact that such a call would appear to be inconsistent with Oswald's having been in Dallas at the time. It thus appeared that the evidence was persuasive that Oswald was not in Dallas on September 25, and, therefore, that he was not in that city at the time Mrs. Odio said she saw him.

In spite of the fact that it appeared almost certain that Oswald could not have been in Dallas at the time Mrs. Odio thought he was, the Commission requested the FBI to conduct further investigation to determine the validity of Mrs. Odio's testimony. The Commission considered the problems raised by that testimony as important, in view of the possibility it raised that Oswald may have had companions on his trip to Mexico. The Commission specifically requested the FBI to attempt to locate and identify the two men who Mrs. Odio stated were with the man she thought was Oswald. In an effort to do that the FBI located and interviewed Manuel Ray, a leader of JURE who confirmed that Mrs. Odio's parents were political prisoners in Cuba, but stated that he did not know anything about the alleged Oswald visit.739 The same was true of Rogelio Cisneros, a former anti-Castro leader from Miami who had visited Mrs. Odio in June of 1962 in connection with certain anti-Castro activities. Additional investigation was conducted in Dallas and in other cities in search of the visitors to Mrs. Odio's apartment. Mrs. Odio herself was reinterviewed.

On September 16, 1964, the FBI located Loran Eugene Hall in Johnsandale Calif. Hall has been identified as a participant in numerous anti-Castro activities. He told the FBI that in September of 1963 he was in Dallas, soliciting aid in connection with anti-Castro activities. He said he had visited Mrs. Odio. He was accompanied by Lawrence Howard, a Mexican-American from East Los Angeles, and one William Seymour from Arizona. He stated that Seymour is similar in appearance to Lee Harvey Oswald; he speaks only a few words of Spanish, as Mrs. Odio had testified one of the men who visited her did. *While the FBI had not yet completed its investigation into this matter at the time the report went to press,* the Commission has concluded that Lee Harvey Oswald was not at Mrs. Odio's apartment in September of 1963.

Note the subtlety at work here. The WC did not explicitly conclude that it was Hall, Howard and Seymour who visited Odio but it certainly strongly implied that that was the explanation, noting that Seymour "is similar in appearance to Oswald," and therefore implying, without quite stating, that it was just a case of mistaken identity: Odio mistook Seymour for Oswald.

But the WC's proposed "solution" to the Odio mystery raised more questions than it answered. Consider that Odio testified that Leopoldo had called the American Leon Oswald. So if the American was Seymour, an Oswald look-alike, Leopoldo (whether it be Hall or Howard?) was deliberately misrepresenting his identity. It was not just a case of mistaken identity. And of course the WC "solution" did not address the most significant issue: the statement attributed to Oswald in Leopoldo's follow up phone call about Kennedy being killed.

But it was not Seymour, and the FBI *knew t*hat if not before the Warren Commission Report "went to press" at least before it was publicly released on September 24th. But as we note below, six days before the Warren Commission Report was published, William Seymour, the supposed Oswald look-alike, told the FBI that he had never visited Odio. We discuss the chronology of the eleventh-hour FBI investigation of the Odio story below. Also note that the WCR does not disclose the association of Hall, Howard and Seymour with the Interpen organization. It is possible that the FBI never made this association, although it certainly should have.

THE CHRONOLOGY OF THE ODIO INVESTIGATION

Although the WC surely recognized the importance of the Odio incident, it issued its report and closed its books before the FBI had completed its investigation of the incident. And when the FBI concluded that Odio's visitors were not in fact the three men from Interpen the Commission did nothing to report that to the public. The public was led to believe that the WC had solved the mystery of the visitors at Odio's door. A disgrace.

If anything demonstrates that the WCR was a rush to judgment (as Mark Lane characterized it), it would be the WC's handling of the Odio incident. Consider the chronology of events in the FBI investigation. On September 18th (a full six days before the Warren Commission Report was released,) the FBI located William Seymour and interviewed him. He denied he had been in Dallas any time in September of 1963. Five days later, on September 23, a day before the WCR was published, the FBI interviewed Laurence Howard and he too denied he had ever visited Sylvia Odio. When the FBI then reinterviewed Hall, he then stated that he had not been in Dallas with Seymour but with a Cuban friend and that he no longer recalled any contact with Odio. Finally, on October 1st the FBI interviewed Odio and showed her photos of Hall, Howard and Seymour and she denied that any of them were among the three that visited her.

Thus, six days before the WCR was released, the FBI had Seymour's denial that he had ever visited Odio. And only one week after the Warren Commission issued its report, the FBI had effectively and finally demonstrated that it had not been

Hall, Howard and Seymour who had visited Odio despite the clear implications of the WCR.

The Warren Commission could have issued a supplemental report or even a press release that what it wrote in its Report about the Odio visitors was wrong, or "no longer viable" to use the language employed by Richard Nixon's press secretary.

It is submitted that given the importance of the Odio affair, the Warren Commission should never have "closed shop" before the FBI investigation was complete. And once the FBI had demolished the Hall-Howard-Seymour story it should have continued its investigation. When the HSCA investigated the Odio story it showed her a whole series of photographs of anti-Castro activists (she was unable, or perhaps unwilling, to identify any of them).

Here is what the House Select Committee on Assassinations wrote about the Odio incident and what a contemporaneous investigation could have done had it been made in 1963 or 1964:

Unfortunately, the nature of the incident makes it, from an investigative standpoint, particularly susceptible to the erosive effects of time. The canvassing, for instance, of both pro-Castro and anti-Castro groups in Dallas, New Orleans, and Miami in search of descriptive similarities to the men who visited Odio might have been fruitful at the time; today it is impractical. The construction of a composite sketch of the individuals when their features were still fresh in Odio's memory might have provided productive evidence 15 years ago; today it is of questionable value considering the natural adulteration of recall over that period of time. A search for the car that the men were driving might have been very productive at the time; today it is useless. The committee was, therefore handicapped by the limitations of the initial investigation and the paucity of evidence developed. The valid investigative approaches remaining were distressingly limited. Nevertheless, because of the potential significance of the Odio incident to a possible conspiracy in the Kennedy assassination, the committee decided that, in addition to pursuing any substantive leads it possible could, it would also attempt to verify the record regarding Silvia Odio's credibility and the details of her allegations.

J. Timothy Gratz and Mark Howell

THE HOUSE SELECT COMMITTEE ON ASSASSINATIONS INVESTIGATES THE ODIO INCIDENT

In 1977-1978, the HSCA investigated the Odio incident. Below is a summary of the HSCA investigation.

Loran Hall testified to the HSCA in executive session (meaning it was closed to the public) on October 5, 1977. His testimony was pursuant to a grant of immunity. Hall denied ever telling the FBI that he had seen Odio with Howard and Seymour, contrary to the original FBI report of its interview with him. In fact he testified to the HSCA that he had never met her.

The HSCA staff interviewed Seymour on November 7, 1977 (i.e. he did not testify under oath). He acknowledged his relationship with Hall and Howard but did not recall any details of taking a trip to Dallas with them. Staff also interviewed Howard on May 23, 1978. He stated he had never met a Silvia Odio.

The HSCA concluded that contrary to the WCR, Odio's testimony was "essentially credible." It went on that "there was a strong probability that one of the men "appeared to be Lee Harvey Oswald." Of course these are weasel words. It could have simply stated that there was a strong probability that one of the men *was* Oswald.

WAS THE ODIO INCIDENT PROOF OF THE PLOT?

Those who posit that the Odio incident was proof of a conspiracy would assert that, whether or not Oswald was with the two Hispanics who came to Odio's door, their purpose was to link Oswald to the assassination by attributing to him the statement about killing Kennedy, which he presumably never made. But there are problems with this scenario

The HSCA stated this about the implications of Oswald's visit to Odio: "No conclusions about the significance of the visit could be concluded." Your authors fully agree with that statement, for the reasons set forth below. However, the HSCA suggested that perhaps Oswald wanted to establish a relationship with JURE so he could implicate that organization, which was left-of-center, in the Kennedy assassination. This is a theory that has also been advanced by others who do not think, as the HSCA did, that Oswald was the (a?) shooter. We respectfully suggest that theory makes no sense whatsoever. The purpose of the assassination was to discredit a left-wing, anti-Communist organization? Nonsense.

Here is why we disagree that the Odio incident was proof of a plot to kill the President. First, although the statement attributed to Oswald by Leopoldo talked about killing Kennedy, he never stated that *he* had any plans to kill Kennedy. His comment was that the Cuban exiles should have done so in retaliation for Kennedy's "betrayal" at the Bay of Pigs.

Second, as we mentioned at the outset, Oswald's association with two supposedly anti-Castro Hispanics flew in the face of the WC theory that Oswald was a Castro supporter and a loner.

Third, if Leopoldo was in fact part of a plot to link Oswald to the assassination, he took a huge risk in attributing the violent anti-Kennedy thoughts of Oswald to a lady he had never previously met. What if she had gone to the authorities immediately and reported that Oswald was talking about killing Kennedy? An FBI investigation might have caused the entire plot to unravel. If Leopoldo was part of the plot, how could he be certain that Odio would not have immediately contacted the police and blown everything apart? We submit that if even an arch Obama critic heard a statement implying that someone intended to kill the President, he would report the threat to the authorities.

Fourth, those who assert that the Odio incident proved a conspiracy ignore the possibility that Oswald had indeed made the statements attributed to him by Leopoldo. That possibility is not inconsistent with the WC theory that he was a lone gunman. Why could a man harboring thoughts about killing Kennedy on his own not make anti-Kennedy statements to his associates?

What is inconsistent however is his association with anti-Castro activists. Moreover, in his statement Oswald never suggested that he was going to kill Kennedy anyway. *It was almost a challenge to anti-Castro activists why they had not shot Kennedy.*

This scenario goes along with another theory of Oswald's role that may surprise many readers: a theory that

Oswald was acting as an agent provocateur working to flush out those who really harbored violent sentiments against Kennedy. What better way to surface such individuals than to have a self-proclaimed marksman make remarks that anti-Castro Cubans should have killed Kennedy? Oswald could have been playing the same role when he visited Mexico City and talked about killing Kennedy for Castro, hoping that he would be contacted by Castro supporters who wanted to see JFK dead. Later we will see what one of Odio's visitors said about "Oswald's game."

Another theory we first heard from researcher Shirrel Rhoades is that Oswald did make the statement attributed to him but he did so to ingratiate himself with Leopoldo and Angel who obviously hated Castro so he could infiltrate their organization. But Rhoades' theory was not new. In the book "Oswald's Game," Jean Davison (an anti-conspiracy writer) made just that suggestion, that Oswald may have been attempting to "infiltrate" the anti-Castro camp with which Leopoldo and Angel were associated. Davidson relates this to Oswald's earlier unsuccessful attempt to infiltrate the anti-Castro group known as the DRE (its full name was the Directprio Revolucinario Estudiantil). We discuss Oswald's important August 1963 confrontation with the DRE in Chapter Three. As we note there, Oswald's unsuccessful attempt to infiltrate the DRE occurred in early August of 1963, less than two months before his alleged meeting with Odio, Leopoldo and Angel.

And the DRE was not the only anti-Castro organization that Oswald attempted to infiltrate. In December of 1962 Oswald attempted to ingratiate himself with members of

Hemming's Interpen organization until he was rebuffed by Hemming. See Chapter Four, "Oswald Attempts to Infiltrate Interpen."

If the theory of infiltration is correct, the next obvious question is Oswald's purpose. Was Oswald attempting to infiltrate these groups (a) on his own personal agenda, whatever that might be; (b) on behalf of the Cuban government; or (c) on behalf of the FBI or CIA? We would dismiss that he was acting on or for the Cuban government and suggest that he was working on behalf of either the FBI or CIA, most likely the FBI. (As noted in Chapter Three, when Oswald was imprisoned following his street confrontation with the DRE he asked to see a specific FBI agent.)

In summary, there are many reasons why the Odio incident, while significant, does not constitute proof of any plot to kill Kennedy, contrary to the argument of many assassination writers.

HEMMING IDENTIFIES ODIO'S VISITORS

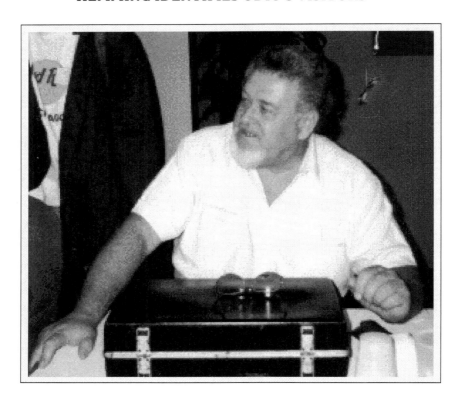

**HEMMING AT DALLAS RESEARCHERS CONFERENCE
November 22, 1995**

At an assassination researcher's conference in Dallas in November of 1995, Gerry Patrick Hemming Hemming indicated that he knew who Odio's visitors were but he was not yet prepared to disclose their identities. He did drop a hint that the man known as Angelo had once saved his life.

J. Timothy Gratz and Mark Howell

Of course Tim Gratx had asked Hemming during the course of his two-year interaction with him about the Odio incident but he always refused comment, stating "Not yet" (or words to that effect).

But then, In the summer of 2007, Hemming disclosed the identities of Angelo and Leopoldo to three writers: myself, Tim Gratz; my fellow Key West author Mark Howell, editor of "Solares Hill" (the weekly literary journal of the Key West Citizen); and author Joan Mellen.

Their identities were first disclosed in print in an article written by Gratz and Howell that was published in a summer 2007 edition of "Solares Hill." Shortly after we published, their names were also disclosed in Joan Mellen's 2007 book "A Farewell to Justice." Mellen actually interviewed "Angel" in the presence of Hemming.

Hemming has stated that he believes that Odio was a spy for Castro. Not because she favored Castro but because she was hoping for favorable treatment or even release of her parents who were still imprisoned in Cuba. So she may well have been feeding information to Castro through one of his agents in Dallas.

According to Hemming, the man who was introduced to Odio as "Angelo" was a Cuban exile named Angelol Murgado. This was the man who had saved his life. Unfortunately we never learned from Hemming the circumstances when Murgado saved his life.

Angelo, born in Cuba in 1939, emigrated to the United States when he was seventeen. When Castro seized power in 1959, Murgado joined the fight to overthrow him. He joined Brigade 2506 in February of 1961 and in April he participated in the Bay of Pigs, was captured and imprisoned in Cuba until JFK ransomed the prisoners in December of 1962.

Rather than being a Kennedy-hater, as many of the exiles were, Angelo was such a supporter of the Kennedys that after Bobby was assassinated in 1968, he changed his name to Angelo Kennedy. According to the book "Live by the Sword," when Manuel Artime visited JFK in the White House in January of 1963, he was accompanied by Murgado, who waited in the White House anteroom. This information came from an interview that Murgado gave to author Gus Russo. Murgado was introduced to Russo by our friend Gerry Hemming. Artime told Murgado that the subject of his discussion with the President was his authorization for a second invasion of Cuba when the time was right.

One author, Lamar Waldron, argued in his book "Ultimate Sacrifice" that there was a top-secret plan for that second invasion of Cuba in December of 1963. A top-level CIA source once stated that had JFK not been assassinated Castro would have been removed from power by Christmas 1963. As one Cuban exile leader put it, their dreams for a free Cuba died with Kennedy on the streets of Dallas.

Artime was a favorite exile of the Kennedys and it was Artime who presented the Cuban flag to JFK when JFK welcomed to the U.S. the members of Brigade 2506 (the Bay of Pigs prisoners that the Kennedy administration had "ransomed" from Castro for $50 million in medical supplies) at a rally in Miami's Orange Bowl in December of 1963 Kennedy promised the Bowl filled to capacity with Cuban exiles that one day the flag would again fly over a free Cuba.

MANUEL ARTIME WITH JFK AT ORANGE BOWL RALLY
DECEMBER 29, 1962

JFK Assassination Unraveled: Book I

BERNARDO DE TORRES
WHO VISITED ODIO WITH MURGADO

Hemming also revealed to us that the man who identified himself to Odio as "Leopoldo" was in fact a high-level Cuban exile named Bernardo de Torres. De Torres was the head of intelligence for Brigade 2506 and he was captured during the Bay of Pigs invasion and he too was jailed until the Brigade prisoners were ransomed by the Kennedy administration in December of 1962.

When author Joan Mellen interviewed Murgado, he confirmed that, as Hemming had reported, he had visited Odio and that he was accompanied by Bernardo deTorres, who used the name "Leopoldo." Angel used his own first name with Odio. In her deposition to the Warren Commission, Odio described "Angel" as being somewhat short and stocky, a description which fits Murgado. Odio described "Leopoldo" as being tall (about six feet) and thin, a description that fits deTorres.

But Murgado threw a definite twist in the Odio story. He told Mellen that when he and deTorres arrived at Odio's apartment, Oswald was already there. They did not bring Oswald to Odio. Thus, according to Murgado, Odio already knew Oswald! In one sense, this stands the Odio incident on its head. It also means that Odio gave perjured testimony both to the WC and to the HSCA.

J. Timothy Gratz and Mark Howell

Robert F Kennedy was concerned that some of the anti-Castro Cubans might harbor violent intentions toward the President. According to Murgado, he was asked by RFK to investigate these concerns. During the course of his investigation he became aware of the activities of Oswald in New Orleans. But he was informed that Oswald was working as an undercover agent for the FBI. Murgado believed that RFK had seen a newspaper photo of Oswald passing out pro-Castro literature in New Orleans. Thus, after the assassination when RFK saw the pictures of Oswald in custody he may well have recognized him from the photo he had seen of Oswald in New Orleans.

A RORKE-SULLIVAN CONNECTION TO OSWALD?

From the HSCA report re the Odio incident:

... No definition conclusion on the date of the visit [to Odio] could be reached. The possibility that it could be as early as September 24, the morning of which Oswald was seen in New Orleans, exists. The visit was more likely on September 25, 26 or 27. If it were, then judging from evidence developed by the Warren Commission and this committee, Oswald had to have access to private transportation to get to Dallas from New Orleans, a situation that suggests possible conspiratorial involvement.

We discuss here how Oswald might have gotten to Dallas from New Orleans—by private air travel. But we should begin by noting that even if Oswald had private transportation, that is, he had someone who flew him or drove him from New Orleans to Dallas, there is no basis for therefore concluding that Oswald's pilot or driver was a conspirator. In other words, if Oswald had transportation assistance that fact by itself does not indicate conspiracy. But it would have been important to determine who was associating with Oswald so close to the assassination.

Hemming linked the mysterious disappearance of Alexander Rorke and Geoffrey Sullivan to the Odio incident. We suspect few readers have heard the fascinating but tragic story of Alexander Rorke and Geoffrey Sullivan.

Rorke, who had been involved in military intelligence in WWII, was an attorney and strong anti-Castro activist who was linked to an early assassination plot against Castro. He was married to the daughter of Sherman Billingsley, the owner of the tony Stork Club in Manhattan. The Stork Club was a favorite nightspot of Hollywood celebrities, politicians and writers, including Marilyn Monroe and Joe DiMaggio, Ernest Hemmingway and many others.

SENATOR JACK KENNEDY CELEBRATES HIS BIRTHDAY AT THE STORK CLUB

There is also available on-line a photo of JFK at the Stork Club in February 1944 with his date Florence Pritchett. Pritchett later married Earl E. T. Smith, whom Eisenhower appointed U.S. Ambassador to Cuba. Smith was a Palm Beach neighbor of Joseph Kennedy. There are stories that JFK remained close friends with Flo even after her marriage to Smith.

As noted, the WCR stated that the only way Oswald could have been at Odio's door and still have made his connections to Mexico City is if he had had private transportation to Dallas, a conclusion shared by the HSCA. The FBI even checked to see if Oswald had been a passenger on a commercial airline flight. But it never considered whether Oswald could have used private plane transportation.

PILOT GEOFFREY SULLIVAN: DID HE FLY OSWALD TO DALLAS TO SEE ODIO?

Pictured is Geoffrey Sullivan, the friend of, and pilot for, Alexander Rorke. We met Sullivan's daughter Sheree at a luncheon on Little Palm Island sponsored by researcher Gordon Winslow of Miami. She successfully sued Cuba for her father's death. Cuba never defended the suit.

Rorke and Sullivan were long-time anti-Castro activists. Space considerations necessitate only the most abbreviated summary of their activities. On December 19, 1961 Rorke, together with Frank Fiorini (who later changed his name to Frank Sturgis and gained infamy as a Watergate burglar) were involved in an operation that dropped over 250,000 anti-Castro leaflets into Cuba. On April 25, 1963, with Sullivan as his pilot, Rorke conducted a bombing raid on a refinery near Havana.

Their activities caused the FBI to confiscate Sullivan's plane.

On September 24, Sullivan filed a flight plan stating their destination was Panama. Sullivan and Rorke left the Fort Lauderdale airport that afternoon in a rented twin-engine Beechcraft. On board as a passenger was a Cuban named Enrique Molina Garcia.

When they refueled in Cozmuzel, Mexico Sullivan amended the flight plan to make Honduras their final destination. That was the last time they were ever seen.

Hemming told us that Sullivan and Rorke met Oswald in New Orleans and flew him to Dallas. We are unsure whether to believe Hemming's story that Rorke and Sullivan flew Oswald to Dallas. For one thing, Hemming never disclosed how he found that out. Obviously not by talking to Rorke or Sullivan. From Murgado's version of events, it does not appear that Murgado knew how Oswald got to Odio's. From whom then could Hemming have received this information? Certainly not from Oswald.

Moreover, when Hemming discussed the Rorke/Sullivan story with A. J. Weberman, he told Weberman that their plane landed at St. Julian base in Cuba where they were killed. He attributed their fate to the fact that they had on their plane the Cuban who Hemming identified as a Castro agent. He never mentioned to Weberman what he later said about Sullivan and Rorke flying Oswald to Dallas for a meeting with Odio.

If Rorke and Sullivan were Oswald's air chauffeurs, as Hemming claimed, it is possible they were recruited by a person who was running Oswald. That scenario cannot be summarily dismissed. And it is not necessarily inconsistent with what Hemming told Weberman.

If Rorke and Sullivan were associated with Oswald, might that association have anything to do with their disappearance?

Although Hemming's version of events has an interesting fit with the timing of the Rorke/Sullivan flight and their disappearance (that is, the whereabouts of Rorke and Sullivan are unknown for the specific time period when Oswald may have used private transportation to get to Dallas) we tend to discredit it for the reasons stated.

There are at least two other pilots connected with the events leading to the assassination who might have served as a pilot for Oswald. And one of them, David Ferrie, had close connections with a Mafia leader who we and many believe was one of the authors of the assassination plot.

Ferrie was the pilot for New Orleans Mafia chief Carlos Marcello. It has been reliably reported that Ferrie met Oswald when Oswald, as a teen-ager, joined the Civil Air Patrol chapter of which Ferrie was a leader. In fact, there is a photograph of the two of them together at a CAP meeting

Many, including your authors, believe that Marcello was one of the masterminds of the assassination. And as discussed above, so did Robert Kennedy.

Ferrie's movements after the assassination were suspicious and were being investigated by Garrison. As the Garrison investigation was heating up, Ferrie was found dead under mysterious circumstances. That is, there were questions if he died of natural causes, committed suicide or was murdered.

Another potential Oswald pilot could have been Howard K. Davis, a close friend of Hemming. Davis, together with Hemming, became involved with the search for the wreckage of the Sullivan/Rorke plane. They were hired by Miami attorney Ellis Rubin, who represented the plane's insurance company, and they spent a week flying over the mountains of Central America looking for the plane.

Rubin, who once represented former Key West police captain Ray Peterson, had a subsequent involvement in the aftermath of the case. He represented CIA spy/Watergate burglar Howard Hunt who sued a publication for its claim that he was involved in the assassination. Rubin won the case for Hunt but it was reversed on appeal and at the retrial Mark Lane successfully represented the publication.

We have no basis for suggesting that either Ferrie or Davis flew Oswald from New Orleans to Dallas. The only point we make is that Oswald could have used private plane transportation, whether piloted by Sullivan, Ferrie, Davis, or someone else. An issue the WC failed to investigate.

You can use the link below to see an interview with Sylvia Odio:

http://www.youtube.com/watch?v=1am-EkfBcmM

The report of the HSCA on the Odio incident can be viewed here:
http://www.jfk-online.com/odiohsca.html

CHAPTER THREE
AUGUST 1963 OSWALD ATTEMPTS TO INFILTRATE THE DRE

August 5, 1963 was a warm Monday afternoon in New Orleans. Cuban exile Carlos Bringueier was attending his haberdashery store, the Casa Roca, when a young man walked in and started to look around the store. It was obvious to Bringuier that the man was not going to make a purchase, and after a few minutes he approached Bringuier and said he wanted to help in the fight against Castro.

He asked for some anti-Castro literature printed in English. The man identified himself as Lee Oswald and said he had been in the Marines and had training in guerilla warfare and that he was willing to train Cubans to fight Castro. He even told Bringuier that he was willing to go to Cuba himself to fight Castro.

Bringuier told Oswald that his work in New Orleans was limited to propaganda and information and had nothing to do with military activities. Bringuier estimated he spent an hour speaking to Oswald. Bringuier did not trust Oswald, fearing he might be either an FBI agent or a Castro agent, in either case someone who was trying to infiltrate the organization with which he was associated, the DRE.

Bringuier's organization was known as the DIRECTORIO REVOLUCINARIO ESTUDIANTIL (DRE).

Often known in the North American press as the Cuban Student Directorate, the DRE was, in the words of one CIA analyst, "perhaps the most militant and deeply motivated" of all the Cuban exile organizations seeking to oust Castro after the Cuban revolution of 1959. According to a CIA study in October in 1962, the DRE had the largest following of any individual exile group.

The group was formed by Alberto Muller, Ernesto Travieso, and Juan Manual Salvat, young Catholic students at the University of Havana, in February 1960. They protested the visit of the Anastas Mikoyan, the Soviet deputy foreign minister. They battled with pro-Castro activists near the statue of Jose Marti in Havana's Parque Central. Later that spring they were expelled from the University in hearings presided over by Castro's campus enforcer, Rolando Cubela.

In Miami the DRE-in-Exile quickly attracted the support of CIA covert operations officers such as David Phillips and Howard Hunt. (In their memoirs, both men praised the leaders of the DRE. See Phillips's *The Night Watch* and Hunt's *Give Us This Day*.)

In the summer of 1962, the group's leaders were the first to report Soviet missile installations in Cuba to the CIA in the summer of 1962. When these reports were confirmed by photographs from U.S. reconnaissance planes, the Cuban Missile Crisis resulted.

As discussed below, the DRE was heavily funded by the CIA.

Oswald returned to Bringuier's the next day, August 6th, with his Marine training manual but once again Bringuier rebuffed him.

Four days later a friend came into Bringuier's store and advised him that someone was distributing pro-Castro literature on Canal Street. Bringuier went with his friend to check it out and was amazed to discover that the man distributing the pro-Castro literature was the same Lee Oswald who just four days earlier claimed he was so anti-Castro he was willing to travel to Cuba and personally join the guerillas fighting Castro. An angry confrontation ensued, that came close to Bringuier hitting Oswald. The police arrived and arrested both Oswald and the Cubans.

The Cubans were soon released on bail but Oswald spent the night in jail. Interestingly, while in jail Oswald asked to speak to an FBI agent.

Bringuier's testimony to the Warren Commission can be found in Volume X of the Commission hearings, which is available on-line.

There is an obvious similarity between what Oswald told Bringuier and what he allegedly told Leopoldo. This similarity suggests that Davison's thesis may well be right: that Oswald's "game" was in fact an attempt to infiltrate these groups, and that in Dallas he was attempting to infiltrate JURE, the group with which she was associated. This thesis, if correct, presumably removes any conspiratorial underpinnings of the Oswald visit to Sylvia Odio. I.e. it had nothing to do with framing Oswald for involvement in the assassination.

We say presumably because it is possible that if Oswald's attempted infiltration was on behalf of, say Castro forces, that the forces behind his infiltration were involved in the assassination. But Angelo Murgado gave an explosive story to author Joan Mellen regarding what Oswald was up to. That follows after we discuss Oswald's attempt to infiltrate two anti-Castro organizations. And even before discussing what Murgado told Mellen it is important to discuss CIA involvement in the DRE.

J. Timothy Gratz and Mark Howell

THE CIA FUNDS DRE AND LATER INSERTS ITS DRE CASE OFFICER INTO THE INVESTIGATION OF THE HOUSE SELECT COMMITTEE ON ASSASSINATIONS

The DRE was heavily funded by the CIA, to the extent of $50,000 per month. The CIA case officer for the DRE was a long-time CIA officer named George Joannides. But the DRE knew Joannides only by his assumed name, Harold Newby.

When the HSCA was investigating the Kennedy assassination in the late 1970s the CIA designated two men to co-ordinate HSCA requests for information, etc. One of the men the CIA so designated was Joannides. But neither the CIA nor Joannides ever advised the HSCA of Joannides' work in 1963 with the DRE. (Of course the HSCA was investigating the possibility that one or more anti-Castro organizations, including the DRE, might have been involved in the assassination. It concluded that none were. But Joannides should have been an HSCA witness.)

Joannides' involvement with the DRE was discovered by investigative reporter Jefferson Morley.

When G. Robert Blakey, former chief counsel of the HSCA, was informed of this, he was outraged, telling Salon magazine: "Joannides behavior was criminal. He obstructed our investigation. In a prepared statement Blakey wrote: "I now no longer believe anything the Agency [CIA] told the committee any further than I can obtain substantial corroboration for it from outside the Agency for its veracity.... " He also stated: "We also now know that the [CIA] set up a process that could only have been designed to frustrate the ability of the committee in 1976-79 to obtain any information that might adversely affect the Agency. Many have told me that the culture of the Agency is one of prevarication and dissimulation and that you cannot trust it or its people. Period. End of story. I am now in that camp." Strong words indeed from the counsel who led the House investigation of the assassination. Blakey confirmed those statements at a 2014 research conference held in connection with the 50th anniversary of the Warren Committee Report.

Morley has an ongoing suit against the CIA to require it to release its documents relating to Joannides' work with the DRE which the CIA has so far refused to do. Its failure to disclose the documents does not, of course, imply that Joannides was in any way connected to the assassination.

Interestingly, however, is the report of Dan Hardway, former assistant counsel to the HSCA, that Joannides seemed intent on delaying and obstructing HSCA requests for CIA documents and information, leading to a possible inference that the CIA deliberately inserted Joannides as one of its primary liaisons with HSCA for purposes of obstruction of the investigation.

CHAPTER FOUR
DECEMBER 1962 OSWALD ATTEMPTS TO INFILTRATE INTERPEN

Oswald's attempt to infiltrate the DRE in early August of 1963 was not the first anti-Castro group that Oswald attempted to infiltrate. In December of 1962 he attempted to infiltrate Hemming's group Interpen and therein lies an interesting tale.

On December 3, 1962, Hemming and twelve of his Interpen members were arrested by U.S. Customs officials led by Cesar Diosdado of Key West. The men were near a boat at Sombrero Beach in Marathon when arrested. The Miami Herald report on the arrest can be found here: http://www.maryferrell.org/mffweb/archive/viewer/showDoc.do?docId=107468&relPageId=2

Diosdado's official title was the Customs officer for Monroe County but he was actually an undercover agent for the CIA; the CIA reimbursed Customs for Diosdado's salary.

Proof of Diosdado's work for the CIA can be found in NARA document # 104-10070-10292 which is a memo from Lawrence R. Houston, General Counsel of the CIA, to J. Walter Yeagley, Assistant Attorney General, Internal Security Division, Department of Justice, dated October 31, 1967. The memo concerns Cesario Diosdado of U.S. Customs and his appearance on a list of prospective witnesses in the case of United States v. Rolando Masferrer, et al.

Diosdado had participated in the arrest of Masferrer and others under a Bureau of Customs warrant. (Diosdado's name is consistently misspelled as Diosado in the document.)

Houston wrote to the DoJ attorney: "As we have informed you, since 1962 Diosado, although carried on the Bureau of Customs roles, was actually working for the Central Intelligence Agency, and this Agency reimbursed Customs for his salary. This arrangement is classified as Diosado's duties were in sensitive intelligence areas and it was not intended that he be known as working for this Agency...."

"If counsel for the defense is able to establish during the trial that Diosado was under the direction and control of the Central Intelligence Agency, it would not only be seriously embarrassing to the Government, but we suggest that it might raise a question of the validity of the arrest in view of the statutory prohibitions on the Agency against the exercise of any police, subpoena, or law-enforcement functions.")

Diosdado arrested Hemming's men armed with the submachine gun he always carried in his car. Hemming told this writer that he approached Diosdado and sneered at him: "What are you going to do, Cesar? Shoot me?" But the Interpen men did not resist arrest and they were taken to the Monroe County jail which was then located on Whitehead Street in Key West. Unlike the current Monroe County jail on Stock Island, the facility on Whitehead Street was not air-conditioned and it was hot, even in December.

Diosdado also confiscated a large group of arms Hemming and his men had been planning to take to Cuba. The charge against them was that they were violating the Neutrality Act, which prohibits private U.S. citizens from taking up arms against foreign nations.

The arrest of Hemming and his followers was reported not only in the Miami Herald but also in the Washington Post.

A day later Hemming was surprised to learn that their bail had been paid by a Miami attorney named Charles Ashmann, with whom he had never had any dealings. Ashmann flew the group to Miami International Airport on his private plane.

Charles Ashmann

An interesting sidebar regarding Ashmann: He received notoriety in September of 1960 when he seized several Cubana airline planes to satisfy a judgment the government of Cuba owed his client, a news agency. One of the planes he seized was the airliner that had taken Castro to New York for a UN meeting and Castro had to hitch a ride back to Havana on Khrushchev's plane.

Hemming told this writer that he suspected the bail had been paid by Jimmy Hoffa in an effort to snub his nemesis

Attorney General Robert Kennedy. That conjecture was never verified and Ashmann is now deceased.

When they arrived in Miami, Hemming's men were besieged by reporters. While he was talking with a reporter, Hemming noticed a man he knew as Lee Harvey Oswald talking to one of his supporters. (Hemming claimed that he had met Oswald years earlier, in 1959, when he was stationed at a Marine base in California.) Hemming instructed his associate to stay away from Oswald.

There is a poignant human interest story to these events. In late December of 1963 a man walked all the way from the fishing lodge on Big Pine Key (which still exists) to Hemming's camp on No Name Key to relay a message to Hemming from his father requesting him to call home. When he did, Hemming's father encouraged, indeed urged, him to return to California for the Christmas holidays. But of course the conditions of his bail prohibited Hemming from leaving the State of Florida.

In early January Hemming learned that his father had passed away. He speculated that his father may have called him because he suspected that death was near. Hemming missed his father so much that he told me that he used to call his father's television repair shop after hours just to hear his father's recorded voice. He almost choked up when he told me this.

The charges against Hemming and his crew were dismissed by a twelve-member jury in June of 1964 when the jury believed Hemming's story that the weapons were intended for a training camp and not for infiltration into Cuba. The weapons were returned to Hemming.

Proof of Hemming's claim that Oswald had confronted his group in Miami is supported by the fact that when Hemming, Attorney Ashmann, and Hemming associate Howard Davis appeared on a Miami radio talk show (WQAM) hosted by Alan Courtney, a man claiming his name was Lee Oswald called the talk show asking to speak to Hemming (who refused to take the call). Shortly after the assassination (on November 27th) Courtney reported the incident to the FBI.

FBI agent Vincent K. Antle interviewed Courtney on November 27, 1963 and this is from Antle's report:

Approximately one year ago, Alan Courtney had Jerry Patrick and three other individuals on his night program on WQAM radio. These individuals were involved with the training of anti-Castro troops. At the conclusion of the program Courtney received a telephone call from an individual who had a very young voice. The young man said he would like to talk to one of the persons who had been on the show. He explained that he was from New Orleans and [was] a former Marine and that he wanted to volunteer his services to be of assistance to them.

Courtney told Antle that the caller "gave the name of Lee Oswald or something like that, such as Harvey Lee or Oswald Harvey or Oswald Lee."

Courtney said that he gave the phone to Hemming's colleague named Davey (that being the name used by Hemming's lieutenant Howard K. Davis). Hemming told us that he'd directed that Davis take the call because he did not want to speak to Oswald.

JFK Assassination Unraveled: Book I

    Hemming confirmed to Key West researcher Shirrel Rhoades that the caller to Courtney had indeed been Lee Harvey Oswald (whose voice he recognized).

    PLEASE STAY TUNED TO FOR THE SECOND BOOK IN THIS SERIES, WHICH WILL COVER MANY OTHER KEYS' CONNECTIONS TO THE JOHN F. KENNEDY ASSASSINATION
    You can write me at tim3056008000@hotmail.com

AFTERWARD

A SERIES OF BOOKS OFFERS NEW RESEARCH

The second book in this new *JFK Assassination Unraveled* series will explore whether Loran Hall may have shot at JFK from the Dal-Tex Building using a Johnson 30.06 rifle that belonged to Hemming. To show what kind of a fellow Hall was, we quote from an interview he gave in May 1977 to A.J. Weberman:

Hall: Who's Gerald Patrick Hemming? Never heard of him. Who is he, some left-winger?
Weberman: He was with Interpen and the International Anti-Communist Brigade.
Hall: That's a Communist organization.
Weberman: The International *Anti-Communist* Brigade is a communist organization?
Hall: Yeah, I wouldn't know anybody like that. Anybody with a name like Gerry Patrick Hemming has either got to be a Communist or CIA.
Weberman: Well, I think this man was a dedicated anti-Communist.
Hall: Who? Gerry Patrick Hemming? If it's the one I heard about he's CIA. I've got nothing to talk to you about. Anybody who associates with Gerald Patrick Hemming has either got to be CIA, FBI or an asshole. I got nothing to say. Hey, nobody is going to print anything I got to say, nobody.

That's fine. I'm in no hurry to get my head blowed off. Hemming is a CIA punk. I've known the son-of-a-bitch for fifteen years. He turned his own goddamned crews in so he wouldn't have to go to Cuba. He has fingered me on my own goddamn deals and caused me to get arrested. Ah fuck. Hey man as it stands right now there's only two of us left alive. That's me and Santo Trafficante.

APPENDIX

TESTIMONY OF SYLVIA ODIO BEFORE THE WARREN COMMISSION

The testimony of Sylvia Odio was taken at 9 a.m., on July 22, 1964, in the office of the U.S. attorney, 301 Post Office Building, Bryan and Ervay Streets, Dallas, Tex., by Mr. Wesley J. Liebeler, assistant counsel of the President's Commission.

Mr. LIEBELER. Would you please rise and take the oath? Do you solemnly swear that the testimony you are about to give will be the truth, the whole truth, and nothing but the truth, so help you God?

Mrs. ODIO. Yes; I do.

Mr. LIEBELER. Please sit down. My name is Wesley J. Liebeler. I am an attorney on the staff of the President's Commission investigating the assassination of President Kennedy. I have been authorized to take your testimony by the Commission, pursuant to authority granted to the Commission by Executive Order 11130 dated November 29, 1963, and joint resolution of Congress No. 137.

Under the rules of the Commission, you are entitled to have an attorney present, if you wish one. You are also entitled to 3 days' notice of the hearing, and you are not required to answer any question that you think might incriminate you or might violate some other privilege you may have. I think the Secret Service did call you, or Martha

Joe Stroud, here in the U.S. attorney's office, called you and gave you notice.

Mrs. ODIO. Yes.

Mr. LIEBELER. Do you wish to have an attorney present?

Mrs. ODIO. No; I don't think so.

Mr. LIEBELER. We want to ask you some questions about the possibility that you saw Lee Harvey Oswald.

Mrs. ODIO. Before you start, let me give you a letter of my father's which he wrote me from prison. You can have it. It was very funny, because at the time he wrote it, the FBI incident happened a week later. I told my father this man had been in my house and he introduced himself as your friend; and he wrote me back in December telling me that such people were not his friends, and he said not to receive anybody in my house, and not any of them were his friends, and he didn't know those people. At the time I did give the names of one or two, and he wrote back, "I actually don't know who they are."

Mr. LIEBELER. Let's come to this during the course of the questioning, but I am glad you brought it up. I do want to get to it, because it may help us determine who these people were.

Mrs. ODIO. Yes.

Mr. LIEBELER. First of all, would you tell us where you were born?

Mrs. ODIO. In Havana, Cuba.

Mr. LIEBELER. Approximately when?

Mrs. ODIO. 1937.

Mr. LIEBELER. How long did you live in Cuba?

Mrs. ODIO. Until, well, I studied in the United States, so I mean--you mean my whole life until--it was 1960.

Mr. LIEBELER. 1960?

Mrs. ODIO. Yes.

Mr. LIEBELER. Then you left Cuba and came to the United States, is that correct?

Mrs. ODIO. Yes.

Mr. LIEBELER. Where did you come to in the United States?

Mrs. ODIO. We first came to Miami, and we stayed there just a few days and left for Ponce, Puerto Rico, and we stayed there 2 years.

Mr. LIEBELER. Then from Ponce, did you come to Dallas?

Mrs. ODIO. From Ponce, I came straight to Dallas last year, March of last year.

Mr. LIEBELER. So that you have been in Dallas since March of 1963, is that correct?

Mrs. ODIO. That's right.

Mr. LIEBELER. You indicated that you had gone to school in the United States. Where?

Mrs. ODIO. Eden Hall Convent of The Sacred Heart, in Philadelphia.

Mr. LIEBELER. How long did you go to school there?

Mrs. ODIO. Three years.

Mr. LIEBELER. That is what, high school?

Mrs. ODIO. That's right. From 1951 to 1954.

Mr. LIEBELER. Was that period of 3 years the only time you were in the United States prior to the time that you came to Dallas in March of 1963? The only time in the United States over any extended period of time?

Mrs. ODIO. Excuse me, when I got married in 1957, I stayed 8 months--9 months in New Orleans.

Mr. LIEBELER. So that you lived in the United States for 9 months in 1956? Mrs. ODIO. That's right.

Mr. LIEBELER. You had been in Philadelphia for 3 years from 1954 on, is that correct?

Mrs. ODIO. No; from 1951 to 1954, when I graduated.

Mr. LIEBELER. And for the period in New Orleans and when you came to the United States finally?

Mrs. ODIO. In 1960, December 25, 1960.

Mr. LIEBELER. So after you came in December of 1960, you went to Puerto Rico and lived in. Puerto Rico for 2 years, and you came to Dallas in 1963 and you have been here ever since?

Mrs. ODIO. That's right.

Mr. LIEBELER. Would you tell us briefly what your educational background is, Mrs. Odio?

Mrs. ODIO. Well, I had grammar school in Cuba. I started high school in Cuba and then I was sent to the Sacred Heart and I applied for college, and went back and studied law in the University of Villanova. I did not finish because my career was interrupted because of Castro, and I didn't finish law.

Mr. LIEBELER. How much training did you have in law?

Mrs. ODIO. I had almost 3 years.

Mr. LIEBELER Of law study in Cuba?

Mrs. ODIO. Yes.

Mr. LIEBELER. My record indicates that on December 18, 1963, you were interviewed by two agents of the FBI, Mr. James P. Hoary and Bardwell D. Odum. Do you remember that?

Mrs. ODIO. That's correct.

Mr. LIEBELER It is my understanding that they interviewed you at your place of work, is that correct?

Mrs. ODIO. Yes.

Mr. LIEBELER Do you remember approximately what they asked you and what you told them?

Mrs. ODIO. I think I remember. Not exactly, but I think I can recall the conversation.

Mr. LIEBELER. Would you give us the content of that conversation, as best you can recall.

Mrs. ODIO. They told me they were coming because of the assassination of President Kennedy, that they had news that I knew or I had known Lee Harvey Oswald. And I told them that I had not known him as Lee Harvey Oswald, but that he was introduced to me as Leon Oswald. And they showed me a picture of Oswald and a picture of Ruby. I did not know Ruby, but I did recall Oswald. They asked me about my activities in JURE. That is the Junta Revolutionary, and it is led by Manolo Ray. I told him that I did belong to this organization because my father and mother had belonged in Cuba, and I had seen him (Ray) in Puerto recently, and that I knew him personally, and that I did belong to JURE. They asked me about the members here in Dallas, and I told him a few names of the Cubans here. They asked me to tell the story about what happened in my house.

Mr. LIEBELER. Who was it that you had seen in Puerto Rico?

Mrs. ODIO. Mr. Ray, I had seen. He was a very close friend of my father and mother. He hid in my house several times in Cuba. So they asked me to tell him how I came to know Oswald, and I told them that it was something very brief and I could not recall the time, exact date. I still can't. We more or less have established that it was the end of September. And, of course, my sister had recognized him at the same time I did, but I did not say anything to her. She came very excited one day and said, "That is the man that was in my house." And I said, "Yes; I remember."

Mr. LIEBELER. Tell us all the circumstances surrounding the event when Oswald came to your house.

Mrs. ODIO. Well, I had been having little groups of Cubans coming to my house who have been asking me to help them in JURE. They were going to open a revolutionary paper here in Dallas. And I told them at the time I was very busy with my four children, and I would help, in other things like selling bonus to help buy arms for Cuba. And I said I would help as much as I could. Those are my activities before Oswald came. Of course, all the Cubans knew that I was involved in JURE, but it did not have a lot of sympathy in Dallas and I was criticized because of that.

Mr. LIEBELER. Because of what now?

Mrs. ODIO. Because I was sympathetic with Ray and this movement. Ray has always had the propaganda that he is a leftist and that he is Castro without Castro. So at that time I was planning to move over to Oak Cliff because it was much nearer to my work in Irving. So we were all involved in this moving business, and my sister Annie, who at the time was staying with some America friends, had come over that weekend to babysit for me. It either was a Thursday or 'a Friday. It must have been either one of those days, in the last days of September. And I was getting dressed to go out to a friend's house, and she was staying to babysit. Like I said, the doorbell rang and she went over--she had a housecoat on--she wasn't dressed properly--and came back and said, "Sylvia, there are three men at the door, and one seems to be an American, the other two seem to be Cubans. Do you know them?" So I put a housecoat on and stood at the door. I never opened my door unless I know who they are, because I have had occasions where Cubans have introduced themselves as having arrived from Cuba and known my family, and I never know. So I went to the door, and he said, "Are you Sarita Odio?" And I said, "I am not. That is my sister studying at the University of Dallas. I am Sylvia." Then he said, "Is she the oldest?" And I said, "No; I am the oldest." And he said, "It is you we are looking for." So he said, "We are members of JURE."

This at the time struck me funny, because their faces did not seem familiar, and I asked them for their names. One of them said his name was Leopoldo. He said that was his war name. In all this underground, everybody has a war name. This was done for safety in Cuba. So when everybody came to exile, everyone was known by their war names.

And the other one did give me his name, but I can't recall. I have been trying to recall. It was something like Angelo. I have never been able to remember, and I couldn't be exact on this name, but the other one I am exact on; I remember perfectly.

Mr. LIEBELER. Let me ask you this before you go ahead with the story. Which one of the men told you that they were members of JURE and did most of the talking? Was it the American?

Mrs. ODIO. The American had not said a word yet.

Mr. LIEBELER. Which one of the Cubans?

Mrs. ODIO. The American was in the middle. They were leaning against the staircase. There was a tall one. Let me toll you, they both looked very greasy like the kind of low Cubans, not educated at all. And one was on the heavier side and had black hair. I recall one of them had glasses, if I remember. We have been trying to establish, my sister and I, the identity of this man. And one of them, the tall one, was the one called Leopoldo. Mr. LIEBELER. He did most of the talking?

Mrs. ODIO. He did most of the talking. The other one kept quiet, and the American, we will call him Leon, said just a few little words in Spanish, trying to be cute, but very few, like "Hola," like that in Spanish.

Mr. LIEBELER. Did you have a chain on the door, or was the door completely opened?

Mrs. ODIO. I had a chain.

Mr. LIEBELER. Was the chain fastened?

Mrs. ODIO. No; I unfastened it after a little while when they told me they were members of JURE, and were trying to let me have them come into the house. When I said no, one of them said, "We are very good friends of your father." This struck me, because I didn't think my father could have such kind of friends, unless he knew them from anti-Castro activities. He gave me so many details about where they saw my father and what activities he was in. I mean, they gave me almost incredible details about things that somebody who knows him really would or that somebody informed well knows. And after a little while, after they mentioned my father, they started talking about the American. He said, "You are working in the underground." And I said, "No, I am sorry to say I am not working in the underground." And he said, "We wanted you to meet this American. His name is Leon Oswald." He repeated it twice. Then my sister Annie by that time was standing near the door. She had come to see what was going on. And they introduced him as an American who was very much interested in the Cuban cause. And let me see, if I recall exactly what they said about him. I don't recall at the time I was at the door things about him. I recall a telephone call that I had the next day from the so-called Leopoldo, so I cannot remember the conversation at the door about this American.

Mr. LIEBELER. Did your sister hear this man introduced as Leon Oswald?

Mrs. ODIO. She says she doesn't recall. She could not say that it is true. I mean, even though she said she thought I had mentioned the name very clearly, and I had mentioned the names of the three men.

Mr. LIEBELER. But she didn't remember it?

Mrs. ODIO. No; she said I mentioned it, because I made a comment. This I don't recall. I said, "I am going to see Antonio Alentado," which is one of the leaders of the JURE here in Dallas. And I think I just casually said, "I am going to mention these names to him to see if he knows any of them." But I forgot about them.

Mr. LIEBELER. Did your sister see the men?

Mrs. ODIO. She saw the three of them.

Mr. LIEBELER. Have you discussed this with her since that time?

Mrs. ODIO. I just had to discuss it because it was bothering me. I just had to know.

Mr. LIEBELER. Did she think it was Oswald?

Mrs. ODIO. Well, her reaction to it when Oswald came on television, she almost passed out on me, just like I did the day at work when I learned about the assassination of the President. Her reaction was so obvious that it was him, I mean. And my reaction, we remember Oswald the day he came to my house because he had not shaved and he had a kind of a very, I don't know how to express it, but some little hairs like if you haven't shaved, but it is not a thick moustache, but some kind of shadow. That is something I noticed. And he was wearing--the other ones were wearing white dirty shirts, but he was wearing a long sleeved shirt.

Mr. LIEBELER. What kind of shirt was it, a white shirt?

Mrs. ODIO. No; it was either green or blue, and he had it rolled up to here.

Mr. LIEBELER. Almost to his elbows?

Mrs. ODIO. No; less than that, just the ends of the sleeves.

Mr. LIEBELER. Did he have a tie?

Mrs. ODIO. No tie.

Mr. LIEBELER. Was it a sport shirt, or working shirt?

Mrs. ODIO. He had it open. I don't know if he had a collar or not, but it was open. And the other one had a white undershirt. One of them was very hairy. Where was I? I just want to remember everything.

Mr. LIEBELER. You mentioned when your sister saw Oswald's picture on television that she almost passed out. Did she recognize him, do you know, as the man that had been in the apartment?

Mrs. ODIO. She said, "Sylvia, you know that man?" And I said, "Yes," and she said, "I know him." "He was the one that came to our door, and it couldn't be so, could it?" That was our first interview. We were very much concerned after that. We were concerned and very scared, because I mean, it was such a shock. This man, the other one, the second Cuban, took out a letter written in Spanish, and the content was something like we represent the revolutionary counsel, and we are making a big movement to buy arms for Cuba and to help overthrow the dictator Castro, and we want you to translate this letter and write it in English and send a whole lot of them to different industries to see if we can get some results. This same petition had been asked of me by Alentado who was one of the leaders of JURE, here in Dallas. He had made this petition to me, "Sylvia, let's write letters to different industries to see if we can raise some money." I had told him too, I was very busy. So I asked and I said, "Are you sent by Alentado? Is this a petition?"

Mr. LIEBELER. You mentioned this Alentado who was one of the JURE representatives here in Dallas. Is that his full name?

Mrs. ODIO. His name is Antonio.

Mr. LIEBELER. Do you know a man by the name of George Rodriguez Alvareda?

Mrs. ODIO Yes.

Mr. LIEBELER. Who is he?

Mrs. ODIO. He is another member of JURE. And at the time, a little after that, after December. I was more in contact with him, and I will tell you why later. They are all members of JURE here in Dallas, working hard. And so I asked him if they were sent by him, and he said, "No." And I said, "Do you know Eugeino?" This is the war name for_ _ _ _. That is his war name and everybody underground knows him as Eugenio. So I didn't mention his real name. He didn't know.

Mr. LIEBELER. Who did you ask this?

Mrs. ODIO. I asked these men when they came to the door--I asked if they had been sent by Alentado, became I explained to them that he had already asked me to do the letters and he said no. And I said, "Were you sent by Eugenio," and he said no. And I said, "Were you sent by Ray," and he said no. And I said, "Well, is this on your own?" And he said, "We have just come from New Orleans and we have been trying to get this organized, this movement organized down there, and this is on our own, but we think we could do some kind of work." This was all talked very fast, not as slow as I am saying it now. You know how fast Cubans talk. And he put the letter back in his pocket when I said no. And then I think I asked something to the American, trying to be nice, "Have you ever been to Cuba?" And he said, "No, I have never been to Cuba." And I said, "Are you interested in our movement?" And he said, "Yes." This I had not remembered until lately. I had not spoken much to him and I said, "If you will excuse me, I have to leave," and I repeated, "I am going to write to my father and tell him you have come to visit me." And he said, "Is he still in the Isle of Pines?" And I think that was the extent of the conversation. They left, and I saw them through the window leaving in a car. I can't recall the car. I have been trying to.

Mr. LIEBELER. Do you know which one of the men was driving?

Mrs. ODIO. The tall one, Leopoldo.

Mr. LIEBELER. Leopoldo?

Mrs. ODIO. Yes; oh, excuse me, I forgot something very important. They kept mentioning that they had come to visit me at such a time of night, it was almost 9 o'clock, because they were leaving for a trip. And two or three times they said the same thing.

They said, "We may stay until tomorrow, or we might leave tomorrow night, but please excuse us for the hour." And he mentioned two or three times they were leaving for a trip. I didn't ask where, and I had the feeling they were leaving for Puerto Rico or Miami.

Mr. LIEBELER. But they did not indicate where they were going?

Mrs. ODIO. The next day Leopoldo called me. I had gotten home from work, so I imagine it must have been Friday. And they had come on Thursday. I have been trying to establish that. He was trying to get fresh with me that night. He was trying to be too nice, telling me that I was pretty, and he started like that. That is the way he started the conversation. Then he said, "What do you think of the American?" And I said, "I didn't think anything." And he said,

"You know our idea is to introduce him to the underground in Cuba, because he is great, he is kind of nuts." This was more or less--I can't repeat the exact words, because he was kind of nuts. He told us we don't have any guts, you Cubans, because President Kennedy should have been assassinated filter the Bay of Pigs, and some Cubans should have done that, because he was the one that was holding the freedom of Cuba actually. And I started getting a little upset with the conversation. And he said, "It is so easy to do it." He has told us. And he (Leopoldo) used two or three bad words, and I wouldn't repeat it in Spanish. And he repeated again they were leaving for a trip and they would like very much to see me on their return to Dallas. Then he mentioned something more about Oswald. They called him Leon. He never mentioned the name Oswald.

Mr. LIEBELER. He never mentioned the name of Oswald on the telephone?

Mrs. ODIO. He never mentioned his last name. He always s referred to the American or Leon.

Mr. LIEBELER. Did he mention his last name the night before?

Mrs. ODIO. Before they left I asked their names again, and he mentioned their names again.

Mr. LIEBELER. But he did not mention Oswald's name except as Leon?

Mrs. ODIO. On the telephone conversation he referred to him as Leon or American. He said he had been a Marine and he was so interested in helping the Cubans, and he was terrific. That is the words he more or less used, in Spanish, that he was terrific. And I don't remember what else he said, or something that he was coming back or something, and he would see me. It's been a long time and I don't remember too well, that is more or less what he said.

Mr. LIEBELER. Did you have an opinion at that time as to why Leopoldo called you back? What was his purpose in calling you back?

Mrs. ODIO. At first, I thought he was just trying to get fresh with me. The second time, it never occurred to me until I went to my psychiatrist. I used to go to see Dr. Einspruch in the Southwestern Medical School, and I used to tell him all the events that happened to me during the week. And he relates that I mentioned to him the fact that these men had been at my door, and the fact that these Cubans were trying to get in the underground, and thought I was a good contact for it, they were simply trying to introduce him. Anyhow, I did not know for what purpose. My father and mother are prisoners, and you never know if they can blackmail you or they are going to get them out of there, if you give them a certain amount of money. You never know what to expect. I expect anything. Later on I did establish opinions, because you can't help but establish opinions.

Mr. LIEBELER. Did you establish that opinion after the assassination or before the assassination?

Mrs. ODIO. This first opinion that I mentioned to my psychiatrist, I did not give it a second thought. I forgot to tell Alentado about it; except 3 days later I wrote to my father after they came, and mentioned the fact that the two men had called themselves friends of his. And later in December, because the letter takes a long time to get here, he writes me back, "I do not know any of these men. Do not get involved with any of them."

Mr. LIEBELER. You have already given us a copy of the letter that you received from your father in which he told you that these people were not his friends, and told you not to get involved with them?

Mrs. ODIO. That's right.

Mr. LIEBELER. Did you tell your father the names of these men when you wrote to him?

Mrs. ODIO. Yes.

Mr. LIEBELER. Your father did not, however, mention their names in his letter, did he?

Mrs. ODIO. He mentioned their war names, because this was the only thing I knew. I probably put an Americano came too, two Cubans with an American, and I gave the names of the Cubans.

Mr. LIEBELER. The copy of the letter that you gave to me this morning, we will mark as Odio Exhibit No. 1.

Mrs. ODIO. He mentioned in the second paragraph, "You are very alone there in. Dallas. You don't have anybody, so please do not open your door to anybody that calls themselves my friends."

Mr. LIEBELER. I have initialed the letter and I would like to have you put your initials under my initials for the purpose of identifying the exhibit.

Mrs. ODIO. Yes, okay.

Mr. LIEBELER. The letter is in Spanish, and you have underlined certain parts of it about three-quarters of the way down, in Spanish. Would you read that translation to us?

Mrs. ODIO. "Please tell me again who it is that calls himself my friend. Be careful. I do not have any friends that have been near me lately, not even in Dallas. So do not establish any friendships until you give me their full names again."

Mr. LIEBELER. Does he say their "full names" in there?

Mrs. ODIO. Their full names again, which means I had given their war names.

Mr. LIEBELER. So you must have given the name Leopold?

Mrs. ODIO. He says, "You are very alone with no man to protect you, and you can be easily fooled." That is more or less what he says. We are 10 brothers and sisters, a big family, and this has been very sad for both of them. I have little brothers in Dallas in an orphanage. We have been, were a very united family, and he is always worried about us being alone after I divorced. He is still more worried, and he was always thinking that somebody could come in my door. He also had a thought that somebody could come by demanding money or something like that. You can probably have somebody who knows Spanish do a better translation.

Mr. LIEBELER. This letter is dated December 25, 1963, is that correct?

Mrs. ODIO. That's right.

Mr. LIEBELER. And it is dated Nueva Gerona. Where is that?

Mrs. ODIO. The capital of Isle of Pines.

Mr. LIEBELER. Your father is a prisoner there?

Mr. LIEBELER. Are the prisoners permitted to write letters back and forth?

Mrs. ODIO. One letter a month, on one side.

Mr. LIEBELER. I would presume that the letters are read by Castro's men?

Mrs. ODIO. They are all read. That is why I did not given him a lot of details. I managed to write very small so they would have a time reading it, like he does. You can see how perfectly he writes a letter.

Mr. LIEBELER. Now, let me ask you how you managed to establish that these men come in late September. You previously stated that you couldn't remember the date exactly, but you had managed to establish it as being in late September. Would you tell me the procedure that you went through to establish that date in your mind?

Mrs. ODIO. I told you my sister Annie was staying with some American friends. She did not live with me. She had gone to live with the Madlocks. And I called her many times to come and babysit for me during certain weekends, and she would come either on a Thursday or Friday, depending on when I called her.

I told her that day that I was going out, but I wanted 'her to start packing for me because we were moving over to Oak Cliff. It must have been the last days of September, because we had already packages in the living room. We had already started to pack to go, and we had to move by the first of October since my rent was due that day, you see.

Mr. LIEBELER. Now, you did move?

Mrs. ODIO. We did move the first of October to Oak Cliff.

Mr. LIEBELER. What was the address of the apartment in which you lived before you moved to Oak Cliff?

Mrs. ODIO. Over in, it was, I am almost sure of the number--1024 Magellan Circle. It is the Crestwood Apartments. I am not sure of the number; I think it is. Mr. LIEBELER. In any event, you were living at the Crestwood Apartments at the time these men came to your apartment?

Mrs. ODIO. That's right. The Crestwood Apartments are full of Cubans.

Mr. LIEBELER. You left the Crestwood Apartments as of the first of October and moved to Oak Cliff?

Mrs. ODIO. That's right exactly.

Mr. LIEBELER. Now, you are absolutely sure that these men came to your apartment before the first of October?

Mrs. ODIO. Before the first of October.

Mr. LIEBELER. It would have been sometime toward the end of September, because you recall that you had already started to pack to move from the Crestwood Apartments to Oak Cliff?

Mrs. ODIO. The packages were in the living room, and Annie was helping me.

She was actually taking things out of the closet when they came. It took a long time to be sure of that, but I am certain of that.

Mr. LIEBELER. Have you discussed this with your sister, Annie?

Mrs. ODIO. We had to, yes, sir; and she was convinced it was in late September. Because she had not come the previous week. For 2 weeks, she had not come, but had come the last week to help me pack and move.

Mr. LIEBELER. Did you have a lease on your apartment, at the Crestwood Apartments?

Mrs. ODIO. No; they don't take you by lease. You give a deposit, and you lose it if you move before 6 months.

Mr. LIEBELER. Had you lived at the Crestwood Apartments 6 months?

Mrs. ODIO. No. I have told you I moved several times, and it is because of reasons of my work, and because my children at the time were in Puerto Rico, I and I went down to get them in Puerto Rico June 29th.

That was exactly the day that I saw Ray again. We had been trying to establish a contact in Dallas with Mr. Johnny Martin, who is from Uruguay. He is from there, and he had heard that I was involved in this movement. And he said that he had a lot of contacts in Latin America to buy arms, particularly in Brazil, and that if he were in contact with one of our chief leaders of the underground, he would be able to sell him second-hand arms that we could use in our revolution.

I don't know if this is legal or illegal, I have no idea. But when he mentioned this fact, I jumped at the possibility that something could be done, because you kind of get desperate when you see your father and mother in prison, and you want to do something for them. So I called Eugenio long distance from Dallas.

Mr. LIEBELER. When was that, approximately? Shortly after you came back from Puerto Rico?

Mrs. ODIO. I think I can give you the exact date. This was before I left for Puerto Rico. June 28, Eugenio arrived from Miami to see Johnny Martin.

Mr. LIEBELER. So you say that on June 28 Eugenio arrived from Miami, is that correct?

Mrs. ODIO. He was supposed to have arrived June 14, but he never did, and I called-two times to make another appointment with Johnny, and he just arrived in time for me to see him. Then it was a time when we met, not Alentado, the other one, Alvareda--Rodriguez Alvareda. So they went to my house. Now, I was living at the time at 6140 Oram Street, the day they arrived. But when I went back to Puerto Rico, the same day, June 29, I saw Ray, and I explained to him what Johnny Martin here in Dallas was up to, and then he said that he was planning a trip also to see if something could be worked out. Mr. Ray himself was planning a trip in connection with that. He was going to Washington to be interviewed by some high official.

Mr. LIEBELER. But he was going to come by Dallas first?

Mrs. ODIO. Yes. So I went to Ponce, Puerto Rico, to get my children, there were four of them, and I brought them back to Dallas. And this is when I moved to Magellan Circle to a bigger apartment, to the Crestwood Apartments.

Mr. LIEBELER. You moved there, after you came back from Puerto Rico with your children?

Mrs. ODIO. I moved there exactly the end of July, the end of the month, because I know when I moved, and then it was in August--let's see, I lived there July, August, and to the last day of September in this Magellan Circle, and then I moved to Oak Cliff.

Mr. LIEBELER. You actually did meet with Eugenio here in Dallas before you went to Puerto Rico?

Mrs. ODIO. Oh, yes.

Mr. LIEBELER. Did Eugenio come to Dallas at any other time after that to meet you?

Mrs. ODIO. No.

Mr. LIEBELER. How many times have you met-with Eugenio here in Dallas?

Mrs. ODIO. Once.

Mr. LIEBELER. That was in June of 1963?

Mrs. ODIO. That's right.

Mr. LIEBELER. So it was not Eugenio who was with Leon when those men came to your apartment?

Mrs. ODIO. No; I would have known Eugenio. He was a very close friend of my family and he did underground activity with my mother and father.

Mr. LIEBELER. Did you ever tell anybody that it was Eugenio who had come to the apartment with Leon?

Mrs. ODIO. No.

Mr. LIEBELER. Do you know Father McKann?

Mrs. ODIO. Yes.

Mr. LIEBELER. Do you remember that he called you on the telephone?

Mrs. ODIO. Yes; he did call me on the telephone.

Mr. LIEBELER. On April 30, 1964?

Mrs. ODIO. The date, I don't recall. Probably.

Mr. LIEBELER. It was approximately the end of April or early May of 1964 when he called you from New Orleans?

Mrs. ODIO. From New Orleans.

Mr. LIEBELER. Do you remember discussing this whole question with him at that time?

Mrs. ODIO. Yes. He asked me if I was withholding evidence of any kind.

Mr. LIEBELER. What did you tell him?

Mrs. ODIO. I told him that everything that I knew I had already told him, and that I didn't know anything else that I could recall that could be important to you.

Mr. LIEBELER. The only time that you were ever interviewed by anybody in connection with this was when Agent Hosty came to your place of work that day, isn't that correct?

Mrs. ODIO. That's correct. But three times I noticed a car standing in front of my door where I live on Lovers Lane. I don't know if it belonged to the Secret Service or the FBI, but I was kind of concerned about it.

Mr. LIEBELER. Did you tell Father McKann that one of the men--did you tell him the names of the men who were there?

Mrs. ODIO. I told him what I knew, the names of the men that I knew.

Mr. LIEBELER. You told him one was Leopoldo?

Mrs. ODIO. Yes.

Mr. LIEBELER. But you did not tell him that you could identify the other man as Eugenio?

Mrs. ODIO. That's right.

Mr. LIEBELER. You did not tell him that?

Mrs. ODIO. No.

Mr. LIEBELER. Now, I have a report before me of an interview with Father McKann by a representative of the U.S. Secret Service in which it states that Father McKann told this Secret Service agent that you had told him that one of the men was Eugenio. But you indicated now that that is not so?

Mrs. ODIO. No. Perhaps he could have misunderstood me, because he has the same problems with names. Probably I did tell him that the man was not Eugenio.

Mr. LIEBELER. Do you remember discussing with him Eugenio's visit to you in June?

Mrs. ODIO. I think I discussed it with him, yes.

Mr. LIEBELER. During that telephone conversation?

Mrs. ODIO. Yes; I think I discussed it.

Mr. LIEBELER. Did you tell Father McKann that the name Oswald was never used in your presence by any of these men?

Mrs. ODIO. Never was used except to introduce me, and the time when they left. They did not refer to him as Oswald.

Mr. LIEBELER. But they did in fact, introduce him as Leon Oswald?

Mrs. ODIO. And I shook hands with him.

Mr. LIEBELER. That is also what you told Agent Hoary when he interviewed you on December 18, 1963, and that is indicated in his report?

Mrs. ODIO. Oh, yes.

Mr. LIEBELER. Now, a report that we have from Agent Hosty indicates that when you told him about Leopoldo's telephone call to you the following day, that you told Agent Hosty that Leopoldo told you he was not going to have anything more to do with Leon Oswald since Leon was considered to be loco?

Mrs. ODIO. That's right. He used two tactics with me, and this I have analyzed. He wanted me to introduce this man. He thought that I had something to do with the underground, with the big operation, and I could get men into Cuba. That is what he thought, which is not true. When I had no reaction to the American, he thought that he would mention that the man was loco and out of his mind and would be the kind of man that could do anything like getting underground in Cuba, like killing Castro. He repeated several times he was an expert shotman. And he said, "We probably won't have anything to do with him. He is kind of 1oco."

When he mentioned the fact that we should have killed President Kennedy--and this I recall in my conversation he was trying to play it safe. If I liked him, then he would go along with me, but if I didn't like him, he was kind of retreating to see what my reaction was. It was cleverly done.

Mr. LIEBELER. So he actually played both sides of the fence?

Mrs. ODIO. That's right, both sides of the fence.

Mr. LIEBELER. Did Leopoldo tell you that Leon had been in the Armed Forces?

Mrs. ODIO. Yes.

Mr. LIEBELER. What did he tell you about that?

Mrs. ODIO. He said he had been in the Marines. That is what he said.

Mr. LIEBELER. Did he tell you that Leon could help in the underground activities in which you were presumably engaged?

Mrs. ODIO. That's right.

Mr. LIEBELER. Have you ever talked to Eugenio about this matter since it happened?

Mrs. ODIO. No, I have not even contacted him.

Mr. LIEBELER. Is your sister Annie in Dallas now?

Mrs. ODIO. She is coming now the end of July.

Mr. LIEBELER. She is not here now?

Mrs. ODIO. No, she is coming from Florida. She is coming to live with me. She spent 6 months with my brother.

Mr. LIEBELER. Can you tell us what her address is in Florida?

Mrs. ODIO. Yes. She is in--wait 1 second--Southwest 82d Place, Miami, Fla.

Mr. LIEBELER. How old were these two men that were with Leon?

Mrs. ODIO. One of them must have been--he had a mark on his face like, I can't explain it--his complexion wasn't too soft. He was kind of like as if he had been in the sun. So he must have been about near 40, one of them.

Mr. LIEBELER. Which one was that?

Mrs. ODIO. But the other one was young. That was the tall one.

Mr. LIEBELER. That was not Leopoldo?

Mrs. ODIO. Yes.

Mr. LIEBELER. Alentado was younger?

Mrs. ODIO. Yes.

Mr. LIEBELER. How old was he, would you say?

Mrs. ODIO. About 34, something like that.

Mr. LIEBELER. Now how old would you say Oswald was? Did you form an opinion about that when you saw him at the time?

Mrs. ODIO. No; I have never thought about it. I mean, I never thought how old he was. He seemed to be a young man. I mean, not an old man. I would say he was a young man; yes.

Mr. LIEBELER. Could you say how old you thought he was after you saw him that day in your apartment?

Mrs. ODIO. I can't say that. I can establish in my thoughts; yes, I could establish an age, but I didn't think of it at the time.

Mr. LIEBELER. What age would you establish you thought about it?

Mrs. ODIO. Oh, 34 or 35.

Mr. LIEBELER. Have you read the newspapers and watched television since the assassination and observed Oswald?

Mrs. ODIO. I read some of it.

Mr. LIEBELER. Did you read how old he was?

Mrs. ODIO. I don't even know what age he is.

Mr. LIEBELER. About how tall was he?

Mrs. ODIO. He wasn't too tall. He was maybe 4 inches taller than I am.

Mr. LIEBELER. How tall are you?

Mrs. ODIO. I am 5 feet 6 inches.

Mr. LIEBELER. So you think he was about 5 feet 10?

Mrs. ODIO. Probably.

Mr. LIEBELER About how was he built? Was he a heavy man or a light man?

Mrs. ODIO. He was kind of a skinny man, because the shirt looked big on him, like it was borrowed.

Mr. LIEBELER. Like it was borrowed from somebody else?

Mrs. ODIO. Yes; that is the impression he gave me, because it kind of hung loose.

Mr. LIEBELER. Didn't fit well?

Mrs. ODIO. It didn't fit.

Mr. LIEBELER. Have you ever had anything to do with the DRE movement here in Dallas?

Mrs. ODIO. Students Revolutionary Council, not at all.

Mr. LIEBELER. Do you know any representatives of the DRE?

Mrs. ODIO. I just knew one.

Mr. LIEBELER. Who was that?

Mrs. ODIO. Sarah Castilo. Now, I have heard about the directorate in New Orleans, because I have family there and they told me about all the incidents about him in New Orleans, about Oswald giving propaganda in the street and how he was down in front of a judge and caused a fight with Carlos Bringuier, and that, of course, this man had been working pro-Castro in this Fair Play for Cuba.

Mr. LIEBELER. Oswald, you mean?

Mrs. ODIO. Oswald.

Mr. LIEBELER. Do you know Carlos?

Mrs. ODIO. Yes; I have met him. I don't think he would remember me, but I know who Carlos Bringuier is. They call him Carlitos.

Mr. LIEBELER. When did you meet him?

Mrs. ODIO. I think it was a long time ago in Cuba, or I was introduced to him.

Mr. LIEBELER. You have never met him here in the United States?

Mrs. ODIO. No.

Mr. LIEBELER. Who in New Orleans told you about this incident between Bringuier and Oswald?

Mrs. ODIO. My family discussed it in New Orleans how he had been handed the propaganda. The other member of the directorate came along, and they had a problem with him, because they were taken in front of a judge. This was true.

Mr. LIEBELER. Have you read about that in the newspapers?

Mrs. ODIO. No; I haven't. This I know from my family, the information we heard from New Orleans.

Mr. LIEBELER. How much of your family are living in New Orleans?

Mrs. ODIO. I have an uncle and a cousin; a married cousin.

Mr. LIEBELER. Which one of them told you about this?

Mrs. ODIO. I think it was my uncle.

Mr. LIEBELER. Were you there at that time?

Mrs. ODIO. Yes.

Mr. LIEBELER. In New Orleans?

Mrs. ODIO. Yes.

Mr. LIEBELER. What is your uncle's name?

Mrs. ODIO. Agustin Guitar.

Mr. LIEBELER. When was this that you discussed this with him?

Mrs. ODIO. February.

Mr. LIEBELER. In February of 1964?

Mrs. ODIO. Yes. I remember that, because I had just come out of an operation.

Mr. LIEBELER. Do you know a man by the name of Joaquin Martinez de Pinillos?

Mrs. ODIO. No.

Mr. LIEBELER. Do you know Emanuel Salvat?

Mrs. ODIO. I have heard about him very much. I know who he is, but I don't know him.

Mr. LIEBELER. Do you associate him with one of the Cuban organizations, Salvat?

Mrs. ODIO. If I have heard something about him, it has been attached to some organization.

Mr. LIEBELER. You don't remember which one?

Mrs. ODIO. No.

Mr. LIEBELER. Would it be the DRE?

Mrs. ODIO. I can't say for sure.

Mr. LIEBELER. Do you know a woman by the name of Anna Silvera?

Mrs. ODIO. I have heard about her, too.

Mr. LIEBELER. Do you have any idea how these three men came to your apartment? Have you ever thought about it and tried to establish any contact that they might have had with someone else that would have told them to come to your apartment?

Mrs. ODIO. They were coming from New Orleans.

Mr. LIEBELER. They came directly from New Orleans to your apartment?

Mrs. ODIO. If it was true. It is very easy to find out any Cuban's in Dallas. Either you look in the phone book, or you call the Catholic Relief Service. If you say you are a friend of so and so, they will give you information enough. They will tell you where they live and what their phone number is and how to contact them.

Mr. LIEBELER. But you have no actual knowledge as to how these men came by your address?

Mrs. ODIO. I kind of asked them, and they told me because they knew my family. That is how they established the conversation. They knew him and wanted to help me, and knew I belonged to JURE and all this.

Mr. LIEBELER. Now, can you remember anything else about the incident when Leon and the two men came to your apartment, or about the telephone call that you got from Leopoldo, that you haven't already told me about?

Mrs. ODIO. No. If I have forgotten something, but I think all the important things I have told you, like the trip, that they were leaving for a trip. And this struck me funny, because why would they want to meet me, if they were leaving for some reason or purpose. And it has been a long time. You don't think about these things every day and I am trying real hard to remember everything I can.

Mr. LIEBELER. Now is there anything else that you think we should know about that we haven't already asked you about in connection with this whole affair?

Mrs. ODIO. No. It would be involving my opinion, but anything that is real facts of the thing, that really happened.

Mr. LIEBELER. Is this the only time you ever saw the man called Leon Oswald?

Mrs. ODIO. The only time.

Mr. LIEBELER. Have you ever told anybody else that you have seen him other times?

Mrs. ODIO. No, I don't think. It would be silly to withhold any information. I mean, the involvement was very slight, and look how much involved you get just from meeting him once. I have a pretty good idea who called the FBI.

Mr. LIEBELER. About what?

Mrs. ODIO. You see, I did not call the FBI to tell them this fact.

Mr. LIEBELER. Why not?

Mrs. ODIO. I was going to, but I had to get around to it to do it myself, because at the time everything was so confused and everybody was so excited about it, and I wanted to wait to see if it was important.

Mr. LIEBELER. Who do you think called the FBI?

Mrs. ODIO. Mrs. Connell, I think.

Mr. LIEBELER. When you were interviewed by the FBI at your place of work, did you have any opinion about the way that interview was conducted?

Mrs. ODIO. Yes. It brought me a lot of problems in my work. The two men were extremely polite and nice, the two gentlemen from the FBI. You know how people were afraid at the time, and my company, some officials of it were quite concerned that the FBI should have come to see me.

Mr. LIEBELER. Have you discussed with Alentado these two men and how they came to see you?

Mrs. ODIO. I never talked to him about it. I decided not to mention anything after the FBI came to see me, because I thought they were going to contact him. I think I gave them the address and the telephone number.

Mr. LIEBELER. You gave that to the FBI?

Mrs. ODIO. Yes. He actually wouldn't know anything about it.

Mr. LIEBELER. You say that because you asked these men if they had been sent by Alentado and they said no?

Mrs. ODIO. That's right.

Mr. LIEBELER. Mrs. Connell that you refer to is Mrs. C. L. Connell, is that correct?

Mrs. ODIO. Yes.

Mr. LIEBELER. How do you know her?

Mrs. ODIO. It is a strange thing. Everything that has happened to me in the past year has been very strange. But I came from Ponce because I was mentally sick at the time. I was very emotionally disturbed, and they thought that a change from Puerto Rico to Dallas where my sister was would improve me, which it did, of course. And I was supposed to see Dr. Cowley in Terrell. He is a Cuban psychiatrist, but he was busy at the time and he couldn't help me. Mrs. Connell belonged to the mental health and at the time she had helped the Cuban group some because they had money, and I was introduced by my sister.

Mr. LIEBELER. Which one?

Mrs. ODIO. Sarita. She actually sent part of the money for my trip to come here to Dallas.

Mr. LIEBELER. Mrs. Connell?

Mrs. ODIO. Yes. So I met her. We became very, very close friends, extremely close, and she talked to Dr. Stubblefield and she got me a psychiatrist, which was Dr. Einspruck. I was here 4 months before I went to get my children. We were close, like I said.

Mr. LIEBELER. What makes you think she called the FBI about this?

Mrs. ODIO. I am not certain of this, but I did discuss this with her after it happened, because I trusted her completely. I discussed it and told her that I was frightened, I didn't know what to do. I did not know if it was anything of importance that I should tell the FBI. And I was the only person--she was the only person I told.

Mr. LIEBELER. Did you tell Dr. Einspruch about it?

Mrs. ODIO. Yes; but the things you talk with a doctor in an office, he will tell you before that he is going to say it. He would have told me, "I am going to tell the FBI." You have to trust a doctor, especially a psychiatrist. I know they talked to him later, but I don't think it was him that called the FBI.

Mr. LIEBELER. Did you tell Mrs. Connell that you had seen Oswald at some anti-Castro meetings, and that he had made some talks to these groups of refugees, and that he was very brilliant and clever and captivated the people to whom he had spoken?

Mrs. ODIO. No.

Mr. LIEBELER. You are sure you never told her that?

Mrs. ODIO. No.

Mr. LIEBELER. Have you ever seen Oswald at any meetings?

Mrs. ODIO. Never. This is something when you talk to somebody, she probably was referring--we did have some meetings, yes. John Martino spoke, who was an American, who was very clever and brilliant. I am not saying that she is lying at all. When you are excited, you might get all your facts mixed up, and Martino was one of the men who was in Isle of Pines for 3 years. And he mentioned the fact that he knew Mr. Odio, that Mr. Odio's daughters were in Dallas, and she went to that meeting. I did not go, because they kept it quiet from me so I would not get upset about it. I don't know if you know who John Martino is.

Mr. LIEBELER. Is that the same man as Johnny Martin?

Mrs. ODIO. No.

Mr. LIEBELER. A different one?

Mrs. ODIO. Yes.

Mr. LIEBELER. Who is he?

Mrs. ODIO. Martino is one that has written a book called "I was a Prisoner in Castro Cuba," and he was on the Isle of Pines for 3 years. He came to Dallas and gave a talk to the Cubans about conditions in Cuba, and she was one of the ones that went to the meeting.

Mr. LIEBELER. Mrs. Connell?

Mrs. ODIO. Yes; and my sister Annie went, too.

Mr. LIEBELER. Did Dr. Einspruch tell you that he had talked to the FBI?

Mrs. ODIO. Yes.

Mr. LIEBELER. About this?

Mrs. ODIO. Yes.

Mr. LIEBELER. Did he tell you roughly what his conversation with the FBI was?

Mrs. ODIO. He told me that they had asked him if I had hallucinations, that I was a person who was trying to make up some kind of story. That was the context of our story. I trusted Dr. Einspruch very much. He always told me the truth.

Mr. LIEBELER. Did he tell you he had told the FBI that you did not have hallucinations and you had probably not made this up?

Mrs. ODIO. Yes. Other people make it up, but--

Mr. LIEBELER. Did Mr. Einspruch tell you he had discussed this question with some representatives of the President's Commission?

Mrs. ODIO. Yes.

Mr. LIEBELER. Did he tell you what that conversation was about?

Mrs. ODIO. He told me that they had talked about an hour and a half about this whole thing, and he told them that he had already told me the whole facts of the thing, and he said let's not mention it any more. You know what we discussed. Don't be afraid.

Mr. LIEBELER. Are you Still seeing Dr. Einspruch?

Mrs. ODIO. No; I am through with therapy. He left.

Mr. LIEBELER. He is no longer in Dallas?

Mrs. ODIO. No; he left for Philadelphia for the U.S. Naval Hospital.

Mr. LIEBELER. Did you tell Dr. Einspruch that you had seen Oswald .in more than one anti-Castro Cuban meeting?

Mrs. ODIO. No; I don't think so, because I have never seen him before except the day he came to the door.

Mr. LIEBELER. You have never seen him since?

Mrs. ODIO. No.

Mr. LIEBELER. You told us before that you had a fainting spell after you heard about the assassination. Would you tell us about that, please?

Mrs. ODIO. Well, 'I had been having fainting spells all the past year. I would pass out for hours, and this was part of my emotional problems. I was doing quite well except that I had come back from lunch, and I can, not deny that the news was a great shock to me, and I did pass out. I was taken in an ambulance to a hospital in Irving.

Mr. LIEBELER. Did you pass out as soon as you had heard that the President had been shot?

Mrs. ODIO. No; when I started thinking about it.

Mr. LIEBELER. Had you heard that Oswald was involved in it before you passed out?

Mrs. ODIO. Can I say something off the record?

Mr. LIEBELER. Yes.

(Witness talks off the record.)

Mr. LIEBELER. At this point let's go back on the record. You indicated that you thought perhaps the three men who had come to your apartment had something to do with the assassination?

Mrs. ODIO. Yes.

Mr. LIEBELER. And you thought of that before you had the fainting spell?

Mrs. ODIO. Yes. Of course, I have "psychiatric thinking." My psychiatrist says I have psychiatric thinking. I mean, I can perceive things very well.

Mr. LIEBELER. What kind of thinking?

Mrs. ODIO. He says I have tremendous intuition about things and psychiatric thinking, which has helped me many times. So immediately, for some reason, in my mind, I established a connection between the two greasy men that had come to my door and the conversation that the Cubans should have killed President Kennedy, and I couldn't believe it. I was so upset about it. So probably the lunch had something to do with it, too, and I was so upset, but that is probably why I passed out.

Mr. LIEBELER. Had you heard the name Oswald before you passed out?

Mrs. ODIO. No, sir. It was only the connection.

Mr. LIEBELER. You had made the connection in your mind between these three men that came to your apartment, and the assassination?

Mrs. ODIO. Yes.

Mr. LIEBELER. Primarily because of the remarks they had made about how the Cubans should have assassinated President Kennedy because of the Bay of Pigs situation, is that correct?

Mrs. ODIO. That's right.

Mr. LIEBELER. You had not seen any pictures of Oswald or heard his name prior to the time of your passing out?

Mrs. ODIO. No; I don't recall – maybe you could tell me what the exact time they mentioned by the radio the name of the suspect. They spoke of a suspect all the time, but they did not mention any name. And I think I came out about 8 o'clock that night. They gave me a shot, so I did not know any name until that night.

Mr. LIEBELER. What time did you pass out?

Mrs. ODIO. I came back from lunch about 5 minutes before 1 o'clock, because we had to punch the clock at 1, and by 1:30 we knew the President was dead, and we all decided to leave, and it was about 10 minutes to 2 that we walked out of the office, and I think I passed out back in the warehouse.

Mr. LIEBELER. Just after you left the office?

Mrs. ODIO. Yes.

Mr. LIEBELER. So it would have been sometime before 2 o'clock or right after?

Mrs. ODIO. Yes.

Mr. LIEBELER. Did these men indicate that they had and come from New Orleans together?

Mrs. ODIO. I am pretty sure that is what he said. Either that they had been, or that they had just come. I cannot be sure of either one, but they had been in New Orleans, or had just come from New Orleans.

Mr. LIEBELER. Would you recognize these men again if you saw their pictures, do you think?

Mrs. ODIO. I think I could recognize one of them.

Mr. LIEBELER. Do you think they definitely took like Cubans?

Mrs. ODIO. Well, this is my opinion. They looked very much like Mexicans. But I might be wrong at that, because I don't remember any Mexican accent. But the color of Mexicans, when I am referring to greasy, that kind of complexion, that is what I mean.

Mr. LIEBELER. When did you first become aware of the fact that this man who had been at your apartment was the man who had been arrested in connection with the assassination?

Mrs. ODIO. It was immediately.

Mr. LIEBELER. As soon as you saw his picture?

Mrs. ODIO. Immediately; I was so sure.

Mr. LIEBELER. Do you have any doubt about it?

Mrs. ODIO. I don't have any doubts.

Mr. LIEBELER. Did you have any doubt about it then?

Mrs. ODIO. I kept saying it can't be to myself; it just can't be. I mean it couldn't be, but when my sister walked into the hospital and she said, "Sylvia, have you seen the man?" And I said, "Yes." And she said, "That was the man that was at the door of my house." So I had no doubts then.

Mr. LIEBELER. Would you recognize this man's voice?

Mrs. ODIO. I don't know. I am not sure.

Mr. LIEBELER. I show you a photograph that has been marked as Bringuier Exhibit No. 1, and ask you if you can identify anybody in that photograph?

Mrs. ODIO. That is Oswald.

Mr. LIEBELER With the X?

Mrs. ODIO. Yes.

Mr. LIEBELER. Do you recognize anybody else in the picture?

Mrs. ODIO. No.

Mr. LIEBELER. I specifically call your attention to the man standing to Oswald's right, the second man behind him, who is facing the camera and has in his hand some leaflets.

Mrs. ODIO. Does he have some glasses on?

Mr. LIEBELER. The man that I just described?

Mrs. ODIO. Does he have any glasses?

Mr. LIEBELER. Let me see the picture.

Mrs. ODIO. He has the same build that that man has in the back.

Mr. LIEBELER. He has the same build?

Mrs. ODIO. A lot of hair here [pointing to the right temple].

Mr. LIEBELER. You are pointing to this man here?

Mrs. ODIO. Yes.

Mr. LIEBELER. You say that his hair appeared to be pulled back in some way?

Mrs. ODIO. One of them, Leopoldo, or the other one. One has very thick hair.

Mr. LIEBELER. You are describing Leopoldo?

Mrs. Ohio. He had hair in front, but he has it pushed back in here.

Mr. LIEBELER. Like sort of a bald spot in his front?

Mrs. ODIO. Yes.

Mr. LIEBELER. Excuse me just a minute, I will be back. Now, you have indicated that the individual standing immediately behind Oswald and to his left, actually in front of the door of this building might look something like one of the men that was in your apartment?

Mrs. ODIO. That's right. That height and that tall.

Mr. LIEBELER. Now, what about the man standing immediately next to him, so we have in the picture starting from the right, a head, and then a man standing in the opposite direction from Oswald, and then we have Oswald, and then we have the individual that you have just referred to about his pushed back hair, or the bald spot in the front, and then we have another man who has a group of leaflets in his hand.

Mrs. ODIO. He looks familiar, but I don't think that was one of the men I saw there at the door. I don't know, Cubans sometimes have the same physique and everything, the narrowness of the shoulders. I mean the back looks something like this man I am telling you about.

Mr. LIEBELER. But you are unable to identify positively anybody else in the picture other than Oswald?

Mrs. ODIO. No; that's correct.

Mr. LIEBELER. Now, I show you a picture that has been marked Pizzo Exhibit No. 453-B, which appears to show a front view of the man with the bald spot, and I ask you if you recognize him as one of the men that was with Oswald in the apartment.

Mrs. ODIO. No.

Mr. LIEBELER. Are you sure that it was not, or you are unable to say?

Mrs. ODIO. No; that man was thinner and a little taller than that picture.

Mr. LIEBELER. Now, you are referring--

Mrs. ODIO. I am referring to this man now.

Mr. LIEBELER. You are referring to a man with the white shirt whose back is toward the camera?

Mrs. ODIO. Yes.

Mr. LIEBELER What about the man immediately behind Oswald?

Mrs. ODIO. No; he was taller than that.

Mr. LIEBELER. Let's refer to this as No. 1. Does it appear to you that the man who is standing sort of sideways to the camera immediately behind Oswald in Pizzo Exhibit No. 453-B is the same man as this man who is immediately behind Oswald and facing away from the camera in Bringuier Exhibit No. 1?

Mrs. ODIO. No; it seems like a different back to me. Actually, possibly the same person, but for some reason, maybe the picture gives trim a slimmer look.

Mr. LIEBELER. You keep referring in Pizzo's exhibit to the man whose back is to the camera with a white shirt?

Mrs. ODIO. Yes; he came with a white shirt.

Mr. LIEBELER. I am having trouble, because I first thought that this man here, who I will mark with the number 1 in Pizzo Exhibit No. 453-B is the same as the man who I will mark as No. 1 in Bringuier's Exhibit No. 1, but it appears that that is not so?

Mrs. ODIO. No; this man is this man in the picture.

Mr. LIEBELER. So we have established that No. 2 in Bringuier's Exhibit No. 1 is the same as the man marked No. 1 in Pizzo's Exhibit No. 453-B?

Mrs. ODIO. Exactly.

Mr. LIEBELER. And the man who we will mark 2 in Pizzo's Exhibit No. 453-B is the man marked 1 in Bringuier's Exhibit No. 1?

Mrs. ODIO. That's right.

Mr. LIEBELER. Now, as far as the man marked No. 1 in Bringuier's Exhibit No. 1 is concerned, you think when you see him there, that might look like the man who was in the apartment?

Mrs. ODIO. He has the same build in the back, and same kind of profile, this side. Here he looks a little broader, and that is not him. It is the same man, but that wasn't the way Leopoldo looked.

Mr. LIEBELER. So the man marked 2 in Exhibit No. 453-B, Pizzo, does not look like the man who was in your apartment?

Mrs. ODIO. No.

Mr. LIEBELER. You cannot in any event recognize the man who we shall mark 3 in both pictures; is that correct?

Mrs. ODIO. Correct. Let me look at that man here [looking]. He wasn't one of them, but he looks so familiar to somebody, this one, the one that has his hand on his face.

Mr. LIEBELER. You indicate that the man who we shall mark 4 in Pizzo's Exhibit No. 453-B looks somewhat familiar?

Mrs. ODIO. Somewhat familiar, yes.

Mr. LIEBELER. Now, I Show you Pizzo Exhibit 453-A and ask you if you recognize anybody in that picture?

Mrs. ODIO. Who is this man?

Mr. LIEBELER. You are referring to the man who we shall mark 1 on Exhibit No. 453-A. Does he look familiar to you?

Mrs. ODIO. The color of him looks familiar. That was more or less the color of that short man. He did not look real white.

Mr. LIEBELER. Does it appear to you that the man we have marked 1 in Exhibit No. 453-A is an oriental?

Mrs. ODIO. Is an oriental?

Mr. LIEBELER. I don't know. Does it look like it to you?

Mrs. ODIO. I don't know. I am just talking about the color of his face, the same color. Now he looks more familiar in this picture, you see.

Mr. LIEBELER. When you say this, you point to the man who we will mark 2 in Pizzo Exhibit No. 453-A, and he is the same man who is No. 2 in Pizzo Exhibit No. 453-B, and No. 1 in Bringuier's Exhibit No. 1? They all seem to be the same man, don't they?

Mrs. ODIO. I think they are all the same man, but for some reason in this picture, he is wearing glasses, isn't he?

Mr. LIEBELER. Well, it looks like it; doesn't it?

Mrs. ODIO. Yes.

Mr. LIEBELER. Did this man wear glasses who was in your apartment?

Mrs. ODIO. Yes.

Mr. LIEBELER. He did?

Mrs. ODIO. Didn't wear them all the time.

Mr. LIEBELER. Now, do you recognize Oswald in any of these pictures; in Exhibit No. 453-A?

Mrs. ODIO. [Pointing.]

Mr. LIEBELER. You indicate the man with the green X over his head as being Oswald, and that is the man who was in your apartment?

Mrs. ODIO. He looks a little bit fatter. I don't know if it is the picture. He looked thinner when he was in the apartment, than he looks in this picture. He was kind of drawn when he was there. His face was kind of drawn. But he looks more familiar there. He looks more like he looked that day.

Mr. LIEBELER. In Exhibit No. 453-B, the man with the green line over his head looks more like the man that was in your apartment; is that correct?

Mrs. ODIO. That's correct.

Mr. LIEBELER. Do you have any doubt that that man with the green line over his head in Pizzo Exhibit No. 453-B Was the man who was in your apartment?

Mrs. ODIO. Well, if it is not, it is his twin.

Mr. LIEBELER. Now, I show you a photograph that has been marked Garner Exhibit No. I and ask you if you recognize that man.

Mrs. ODIO. That is Oswald.

Mr. LIEBELER. Is that the man who was in your apartment?

Mrs. ODIO. Yes.

Mr. LIEBELER. Are you sure?

Mrs. ODIO. He doesn't have the little thing, the little moustache that he had that day. He looks shaved there, and he did not look shaved that day.

Mr. LIEBELER. I show you Pizzo Exhibit No. 453-C and ask you if that looks like the man who was in your apartment?

Mrs. ODIO. That is not the expression he had, but he has the same forehead and everything. But his lips, the only thing that confuses me is the lips that did not look like the same man. It is that unshaved thing that got me that day.

Mr. LIEBELER. Does Pizzo Exhibit No. 453-C appear to you, does the man in that picture appear to be Somewhat unshaven, or similar to the one you saw in your apartment?

Mrs. ODIO. I think he was not. The only thing he had not shaved was around where the mouth is, and everything else was shaved. That is way he looked, kind of clothes hanging on him.

Mr. LIEBELER. Do you think this man in Pizzo Exhibit No. 453-C is Lee Harvey Oswald?

Mrs. ODIO. Yes; I think that is him.

Mr. LIEBELER. Do you think that is the man that was in your apartment?

Mrs. ODIO. Well, let me say something. I think this man was the one that was in my apartment. I am not too sure of that picture. He didn't look like this. He was smiling that day. He was more smiling than in this picture.

Mr. LIEBELER. We have to put the pictures down on the record, because when somebody reads the record-- you say that he--

Mrs. ODIO. He looks more relaxed in Exhibit No. 453-C. He looks more smiling, like Exhibit No. 453-B, or different countenance.

Mr. LIEBELER. I have some motion pictures of the scene that we have been looking at here in these still pictures. These pictures that have been marked Exhibit Nos. 453-B and 453-C were taken from a movie that was made of that, and we also have on that movie a picture of Lee Oswald as he appeared on the television program in New Orleans on a sound track. I want you to look at those pictures and tell us after you have looked at the pictures if you think that man was the same man who was in your apartment.

I have not yet made arrangements for the projector to be set up, and there is an FBI agent bringing another picture over here from the FBI office that I want you to look at this morning before you leave. But I would like to have you--and I have another witness waiting for me, and I have nine more witnesses. Could you come back later this evening to look at the motion pictures? And in the meantime, I will have the Secret Service set up a projection room to view the films?

Mrs. ODIO. Yes.

Mr. LIEBELER. Why don't we terminate momentarily now, and as soon as the FBI comes over, I will show you this picture, and I will call the Secret Service and find out when he can set up the viewing of this film, and I will tell You what time to come back.

Mrs. ODIO. Since I am going to be downtown, do you want me to come back any special time?

Mr. LIEBELER. I will tell you as soon as I talk to Mr. Sorrels.

Mrs. ODIO. Before I leave?

Mr. LIEBELER. I can't tell you before you leave. I will see if I can set up a time. When you say that these men came to your apartment in late September of 1963, can you give me your best recollection as to how long before the first of October they came? You moved out of your apartment in the Crestwood Apartments on the very last day of September; is that correct? Or can you. remember? Is there any way you can check that by finding out when you moved into your apartment in Oak Cliff?

Mrs. ODIO. The day I moved, I had gone to work, so it must have been on a Monday or Tuesday. This man must have come by the end of the previous weekend.

Mr. LIEBELER. I show you a 1963 calendar and point out to you that the last day of September was Monday.

Mrs. ODIO. That is probably the day I moved.

Mr. LIEBELER. Did you say that you also started working at a new job that same day?

Mrs. ODIO. No, sir.

Mr. LIEBELER. But you had been working on the day that you did move?

Mrs. ODIO. I started working initially the 15th of September, because it was too far away where I lived in Irving. I started the 15th of September, I am almost sure of the 15th or the 9th. Let me see what day was the 9th. It was a Monday. It was the 9th, sir, that I started working at National Chemsearch.

(Special Agent Bardwell O. Odum of the Federal Bureau of Investigation entered the hearing room.)

Mr. LIEBELER. This is Mr. Odum from the FBI. As a matter of fact, Mr. Odum was the man that interviewed you.

Mrs. ODIO. I remember. He looked very familiar.

Mr. ODIO. What is the name?

Mrs. ODIO. Odio.

Mr. ODIO. I interview so many people, it slips my mind at the moment.

(Agent Odum left the hearing room.)

Mr. LIEBELER. Now, you have indicated on the calendar, you circled the 30th of September, and you drew a line around the 26th, 27th, and 28th of September. Can you tell me what you meant by that?

Mrs. ODIO. The 30th was the day I moved. The 26th, 27th, and 28th, it could have been either of those 3 days. It was not on a Sunday.

Mr. LIEBELER. Now you indicated previously that Leopoldo called you the immediately following day after they had been there; is that correct?

Mrs. ODIO. That's correct.

Mr. LIEBELER. And you also testified, according to my recollection, that you had been at work on the day that Leopoldo called you; is that correct?

Mrs. ODIO. Yes; it would be the 26th or the 27th for sure.

Mr. LIEBELER. Would you work on Saturday?

Mrs. ODIO. No; but he could have called me Saturday. But they would have come Thursday or Friday.

Mr. LIEBELER. Thursday or Friday?

Mrs. ODIO. That's right.

Mr. LIEBELER. Because you had been at work on the day they came?

Mrs. ODIO. Yes.

Mr. LIEBELER. Do you remember whether you had been at work on the day that Leopoldo called you?

Mrs. ODIO. I don't recall that.

Mr. LIEBELER. You can't recall that?

Mrs. ODIO. No. I know I was very busy with the kids, but I don't remember.

Mr. LIEBELER. I show you a picture which depicts the same individual that is depicted in an exhibit which has previously been marked Commission Exhibit No. 237, and I ask you if you recognize that man.

Mrs. ODIO. No, sir.

Mr. LIEBELER. That is not the man that was with Leon when he came to your apartment?

Mrs. ODIO. No. I wish I could point him to you. One was very tall and slim, kind of. He had glasses, because he took them off and put them back on before he left, and they were not sunglasses. And the other one was short, very Mexican looking. Have you ever seen a short Mexican with lots of thick hair and a lot of hair on his chest?

Mr. LIEBELER. So there was a shorter one and a tall one, and the shorter one was rather husky?

Mrs. ODIO. He was not as big as this man.

Mr. LIEBELER. Not as big as the man in Exhibit No. 237?

Mrs. ODIO. That's right.

Mr. LIEBELER. IS that the man in Exhibit No. 237 that had a pushed back spot on his head?

Mrs. ODIO. It was different. In the middle of his head it was thick, and it looked like he didn't have any hair, and the other side, I didn't notice that.

Mr. LIEBELER. This was the taller man; is that right? The one known as Leopoldo?

Mrs. ODIO. Yes.

Mr. LIEBELER. About how much did the taller man weigh, could you guess?

Mrs. ODIO. He was thin--about 165 pounds.

Mr. LIEBELER. How tall was he, about?

Mrs. ODIO. He was about 3 1/2 inches, almost 4 inches taller than I was. Excuse me, he couldn't have. Maybe it was just in the position he was standing. I know that made him look taller, and I had no heels on at the time, so he must have been 6 feet; yes.

Mr. LIEBELER. And the shorter man was about how tall, would you say? Was he taller or shorter than Oswald?

Mrs. ODIO. Shorter than Oswald.

Mr. LIEBELER. About how much, could you guess?

Mrs. ODIO. Five feet seven, something like that.

Mr. LIEBELER. So he could have been 2 or 3 inches shorter than Oswald?

Mrs. ODIO. That's right.

Mr. LIEBELER. He weighed about how much, would you say?

Mrs. ODIO. 170 pounds, something like that, because he was short, but he was stocky, and he was the one that had the strange complexion.

Mrs. LIEBELER. Was it pock marked, would you say?

Mrs. ODIO. No; it was like it wasn't, because he was, oh, it was like he had been in the sun for a long time.

Mr. LIEBELER. Let's terminate now and we will resume when we show the film to you tonight.

TESTIMONY OF SYLVIA ODIO RESUMED

The testimony of Sylvia Odio was taken at 6:30 p.m., on July 22, 1964, at the office of the Secret Service, 505 North Ervay Street, Dallas, Tex., by Mr. Wesley J. Liebeler, assistant counsel of the President's Commission. Forrest Sorrels and John Joe Howlett, special agents of the U.S. Secret Service were present.

Mr. LIEBELER. This is the continued deposition of Mrs. Sylvia Odio, which is now being continued in the office of the Secret Service. We have made arrangements in the presence of Agent Forrest Sorrels and Agent Howlett, to show some movie films of some street scenes in the city of New Orleans, and also a television appearance that Lee Harvey Oswald made over station WDSU in New Orleans in August of 1963. I want to ask Mrs. Odio to watch the film, and if you recognize anybody in the film at any time say so as you see him and point the individual out and we will run the film backward and see what it looks like at that time. Please go ahead, John.

Mrs. ODIO [viewing film]. The man from the back with the glasses, I have seen him, the tall thin one. I would like to see the beginning where the man started coming in.

(Film was rerun.)

Mrs. ODIO. You see the one with the glasses, that thin man. He doesn't have a mustache, though.

Mr. LIEBELER. That third man there?

Mrs. ODIO. I will show you the back when he comes. The man over to the right in the white shirt from the back, that looks so familiar.

Mr. LIEBELER. That one right over there?

Mrs. ODIO. Right; he has the same build.

Mr. LIEBELER. Can you back it up, John? Let me ask you this now, Sylvia. Did you recognize Lee Harvey Oswald?

Mrs. ODIO. Oh, yes; definitely. He made a television appearance. He looked much more similar than the pictures from New Orleans. He had the same mustache here.

Mr. LIEBELER. In the television appearance?

Mrs. ODIO. Yes.

Mr. LIEBELER. What about in the pictures that you saw in the police station of him standing against the wall when he walked out of the police station, did that look like the man that was in your apartment?

Mrs. ODIO. Yes.

Mr. LIEBELER. What about his voice? Did you recognize any similarity in his voice?

Mrs. ODIO. No. I don't know if it was because in the television it changed, or something, and he didn't speak too much that day, and it is hard to remember a voice after such a long time.

Mr. LIEBELER. After looking at this picture, are you more convinced, or less convinced, or do you still have about the same feeling that you had before you looked at it that the man who was in your apartment late in September was the same man as Lee Harvey Oswald?

Mrs. ODIO. I have to be careful about that, because I have the same feeling that it was, but at the same time I have been looking at papers for months and months of pictures, and these help you to remember too much. I wish I could isolate the incident without remembering the other pictures. I have a feeling there are certain pictures that do not resemble him. It was not the Oswald that was standing in front of my door. He was kind of tired looking. He had a little smile, but he was sunken in in the face that day. More skinny, I would say.

Mr. LIEBELER. Well, do you have any doubts in your mind after looking at these pictures that the man that was in your apartment was the same man as Lee Harvey Oswald?

Mrs. ODIO. I don't have any doubts.

Mr. LIEBELER. Do you want to run the picture once more, John?

Mrs. ODIO. What I am trying to establish is the man with the bald in the back was similar to the profile, but he seems lighter in this picture. But the men looked like Mexicans. They did not look like Cubans.

Mr. LIEBELER. Now we have here two pictures that have been made from films of this movie.

Mrs. ODIO. In that picture he didn't resemble that at all [pointing].

Mr. LIEBELER. You are referring to Pizzo Exhibit No. 453-B; the man marked with the number 2?

Mrs. ODIO. That's right.

Mr. LIEBELER. That is the same man you have been talking about as looking similar?

Mrs. ODIO. That's right. But in the motion picture he looks thinner and I was trying to give you an idea of the man that I saw that day.

Mr. LIEBELER. Do you think that the man you saw in the motion picture, who is the same man marked number 2 in Pizzo Exhibit No. 453-B, could have been the same man that was in your apartment with Oswald?

Mrs. ODIO. I think he had a mustache, and this man in the apartment does not have any mustache.

Mr. LIEBELER. But otherwise, you think that he looks similar?

Mrs. ODIO. They have the same stature and same build and profile. I can say he was standing to the side in the door, and his hair was pulled back on one side.

Mr. LIEBELER. Do you want to run through it again, please?

(Film was rerun.)

Mrs. ODIO. The picture that resembled most, even though his hair was not so cut that day.

Mr. LIEBELER. You have referred to the individual that was walking out of the police station?

Mrs. ODIO. With his back.

Mr. LIEBELER. He had a mustache, and he had glasses on?

Mrs. ODIO. That day he did not have a mustache. He just had glasses, and he would take them off and on. Lee Oswald--Leon is fatter in this picture than what I actually saw him.

Mr. LIEBELER. You think this man standing on the corner, who is No. 2 in Pizzo Exhibit No. 453-B, is the same man you saw walking out of the police station?

Mrs. ODIO. No.

Mr. LIEBELER. It is a different man?

Mrs. ODIO. That's right. The one that is walking out of the door, kind of thin-looking individual, is darker.

Mr. LIEBELER. Is the man that was walking out of the police station?

Mrs. ODIO. You want me to point it out?

Mr. LIEBELER. Yes. Run it back. I think we should indicate in the record there was a confusion in my mind, because I think it is pretty clear that the man that was walking out of the police station is a different man than is in Pizzo Exhibit No. 453-B.

Mrs. ODIO. He looked greasy looking. I will tell you when [looking at film].

Mr. LIEBELER. Is it that man with the sunglasses that walked out of the door?

Mrs. ODIO. That is the picture I see. That picture is what I mean.

Mr. LIEBELER. Yes. There he is again [indicating individual with mustache leaving police station with Carios Bringuier and others depicted on film].

Mrs. ODIO. There he is again; big ears, but from the front, he doesn't resemble it. It is the same build from the back, that thin neck.

Mr. LIEBELER. You think that that man we have Just seen in the picture resembles one of the men that was in your apartment?

Mrs. ODIO. From the back, because I remember that I put the light on on the porch, and I saw them get in the car. I wanted to be sure they were gone.

Mr. LIEBELER. But it is clearly not the same individual?

Mrs. ODIO. No, sir; clearly not the same. I am trying to see something, to put something in paper that would make me remember. [The film was rerun but the witness did not recognize anyone depicted on it except as indicated above.]

Mr. LIEBELER. Thank you very much, Mrs. Odio.

ABOUT THE AUTHORS

J. Timothy Gratz

After graduating from the University of Wisconsin Law School in 1973, Tim Gratz practiced business litigation and medical malpractice for nineteen years before moving to Florida in 1993.

During his student years, Gratz was very active in Republican politics, serving as Chair of the Wisconsin Teen-Age Republicans and later Chair of the Wisconsin College Republicans. In the latter capacity Gratz worked closely with Karl Rove, who was then National Chairman of the College Republicans.

Gratz says his "fifteen minutes of fame" comes from his mention in the Senate Watergate Committee Report.

As it happened, Gratz had been approached by Donald Segretti, a Nixon aide who was running a "dirty tricks" campaign against Democrat candidates. Segretti claimed, in "Mission Impossible" style, that he was working under the "highest authority" but that his superiors would deny any such authorization. Gratz was highly suspicious of Segretti. ("He was acting like he was James Bond, but he came across more like a fumbling Maxwell Smart," Gratz said.) He could not believe that any responsible politician would condone several of the activities Segretti was proposing, so he reported Segretti's approach to the Nixon campaign. According to the book *The President's Private Eye*, no one at even the highest level of the Nixon campaign knew of Segretti's activities until they investigated Gratz's claim and discovered that Segretti was in fact being run out of the White House.

Although Gratz had been an ardent supporter of Barry Goldwater, he was so saddened by the murder of JFK that he cried the entire weekend of the assassination. Like so many others, he became suspicious of a conspiracy when Jack Ruby silenced the supposed "lone gunman", and his suspicions were solidified when in 1966 he read Mark Lane's *Rush to Judgment.* In 2003, he became an amateur "assassination researcher' when he read about the claim of Key West businessman George Faraldo that he had seen Lee Oswald and Jack Ruby together at the Key West airport.

Mark Howell

Mark Howell is a graduate of Cambridge University in Great Britain. He was a legendary figure in London's paperback world before becoming acquisitions editor on the multi-million-copy selling *Mack Bolan: The Executioner* series (soon to be a major movie) when it was purchased by Harlequin Books to launch the action-adventure Gold Eagle imprint.

In Key West, Howell served as senior writer and editor of Solares Hill during its award-winning final decade, becoming a household name with his weekly Soundings column. It was while he worked at Solares Hill for The Key West Citizen that he began collaboration with Tim Gratz that broke new ground in the history of the Florida Keys connections to the Kennedy assassination.

Prior to the 50th anniversary of the assassination, Howell joined with Tim Gratz and Shirrel Rhoades in presenting a well-received seminar at Florida Keys Community College on Lee Harvey Oswald and the events in Dallas of November 1963.

AbsolutelyAmazingEbooks.com
or AA-eBooks.com